101 PLACES TO PRAY BEFORE YOU DIE

D0873163

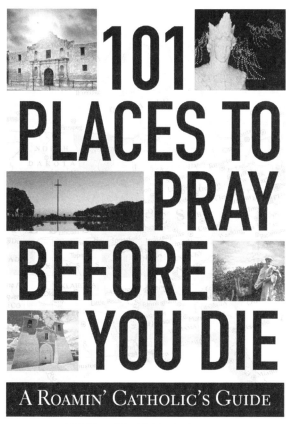

101 PLACES TO PRAY BEFORE YOU DIE

A ROAMIN' CATHOLIC'S GUIDE

THOMAS J. CRAUGHWELL

franciscan
media
Cincinnati, Ohio

LIVINGSTON PUBLIC LIBRARY
10 Robert Harp Drive
Livingston, NJ 07039

The websites, telephone numbers, addresses, and other information specific to each of the sites noted here were current at the time of publication, but may be subject to change.

Cover design by LUCAS Art & Design
Book design by Mark Sullivan

LIBRARY OF CONGRESS CATALOGING-IN-PUBLICATION DATA
Names: Craughwell, Thomas J., 1956- author.
Title: 101 places to pray before you die : a roamin Catholic's guide / Thomas
J. Craughwell.
Other titles: One hundred one places to pray before you die | One hundred and
one places to pray before you die
Description: Cincinnati : Franciscan Media, 2017.
Identifiers: LCCN 2016049546 | ISBN 9781632530868 (trade paper)
Subjects: LCSH: Prayer—Catholic Church. | Sacred space—United States. |
Christian shrines—United States.
Classification: LCC BV210.3 .C735 2017 | DDC 263/.04273—dc23
LC record available at https://lccn.loc.gov/2016049546

ISBN 978-1-63253-086-8
Copyright ©2017, Thomas J. Craughwell. All rights reserved.

Published by Franciscan Media
28 W. Liberty St.
Cincinnati, OH 45202
www.FranciscanMedia.org

Printed in the United States of America.
Printed on acid-free paper.
17 18 19 20 21 5 4 3 2 1

Contents

Introduction

In the late 1980s, I lived in Brooklyn. I had a pretty nice, reasonably priced, one-bedroom apartment, but my neighborhood was, to be charitable, tired. On weekends, there was nothing of interest to keep me there, so I got in the habit of taking the subway under the East River to Manhattan.

The indispensable handbook to planning my weekend escapes was the *American Institute of Architects Guide to New York City*. It gave me an in-depth view of the history of New York City and an in-depth view of the evolution of architecture and design in the city. So I explored historic districts such as Greenwich Village, Murray Hill, Lower Manhattan, and even that tourist mecca, the South Street Seaport, which displaced the old Fulton Fish Market. (It's nice enough in an outdoor shopping mall kind of way, but I say bring back the fish.)

One of the surprises of the *AIA Guide* was the editors' enthusiasm for Catholic churches and shrines in Manhattan. The main reason? When we Catholics build a church or chapel, we tend to fill it with cool stuff. We hire artists, sculptors, wood-carvers, and stained glass designers to make our churches beautiful.

In Manhattan there are many churches that are just plain red brick outside, the kind of place that you might breeze right by without giving it a second look. But the AIA editors instructed me to step inside and see wonderful things, such as the Massive mural of the crucifixion over the high altar of St. Stephen's Church, which was commissioned from the Italian immigrant artist who painted the murals in the US Capitol. I was directed down to the Battery where, from the front steps of the little chapel built on the site of Mother Seton's home, you get a wonderful view of the Statue of Liberty and Ellis Island.

And at Old St. Patrick's Cathedral, up one aisle and down the other I found row upon row of statues of the saints, standing amid banks of real candles. I love Old St. Patrick's, so I'm going to give it a little extra space. For more than two hundred years Old St. Patrick's has welcomed wave after wave of newcomers to America, from the Irish (during the Civil War, the Irish Brigade considered St. Patrick's their spiritual headquarters), to the Italians who gave us the annual Feast of San Gennaro, to the Chinese who attend Mass at the old cathedral today.

I've always liked tracking down the unexpected, and the *AIA Guide* directed my footsteps. One of my favorite walking tours was to the sites associated with Alfred E. Smith, the first Catholic to win the nomination for president (he lost). Smith's old neighborhood, once heavily Irish, is part of Chinatown now, but it still has the feel he would recognize—streets teeming with immigrants, tiny, crowded shops run by entrepreneurs from the old country, and noisy, crazy traffic. So Al Smith's neighborhood has changed, but not really.

I've tried to bring my joy in the unexpected to this book. Yes, among the more than one hundred places to pray in your lifetime, you'll find plenty of cathedrals and churches here, but also destinations that might have gotten away from you. The National Sanctuary of Our Sorrowful Mother in Portland, Oregon, is not only holy ground, it is also home to a splendid botanical garden where every month of the year something is blooming.

Myles Keogh, an Irishman, fought in defense of the Papal States in Italy, then in defense of the Union during America's Civil War, and then with the Seventh Cavalry in the Far West; he died with Custer and all his fellow troopers at the Little Bighorn. According to one story, Keogh was the last cavalryman to be killed by the Native Americans; a white marble marker identifies the place where he fell.

And after you've finished touring some of the grand mansions of Newport, Rhode Island, head over to Salve Regina University. Over the decades the college has acquired the estates of seven of Gilded Age America's wealthiest families; their oceanfront mansions and outbuildings give an extra elegance, even opulence, to the life of students, faculty, and staff at Salve Regina.

Then there are the retreat houses. These days it's fairly easy to find a quiet place to make a retreat, but I've selected houses that offer a little something extra. The Vikingsborg Guest House in Connecticut overlooks the serene Long Island Sound. New Mexico's Monastery of Christ in the Desert stands at the base of a soaring butte, at the end of a fifteen-mile-long unpaved road— you'll need a four-wheel-drive vehicle to reach this place. And accommodations at the Shrine of Our Lady of La Salette in Enfield, New Hampshire, are in the Great Stone Dwelling House, one of the largest residences the Shakers ever built (the La Salette Fathers acquired the land and the buildings in the 1930s when the Shaker community in Enfield was dying out).

Although he was a lapsed Catholic, Irish author James Joyce was once asked to define Catholicism; he replied, "Here comes everybody." I've tried to take that big tent approach in this book by including shrines and historic sites that have special significance among Latino Catholics (the sanctuary of Chimayo in New Mexico), Vietnamese Catholics (Our Lady of Lavang Shrine in Houston, Texas), and African American Catholics (St. Augustine Seminary in Bay St. Louis, Mississippi, the first seminary founded specifically to train and ordain black men to the priesthood).

I've included a driving tour of sites associated with Venerable Frederic Baraga, the aristocratic Slovenian priest and later bishop who worked himself to exhaustion ministering to his largely Native American congregation in Michigan's Upper Peninsula. Even northern Midwest winters couldn't stop him: in foul weather he pulled on his snowshoes and trekked across the drifts to bring the sacraments to his people. In his old age, he made a concession to his infirmities and made the same trips by dog sled.

Especially touching, from my perspective, are the shrines erected by families, such as Our Lady of Ephesus House of Prayer in Jamaica, Vermont, and the monumental statue of Our Lady of Peace Shrine in Pine Bluffs, Wyoming. The heroic devotion and heroic self-sacrifice of these families is inspiring.

My goal here is to introduce you to great Catholic sites that you might have overlooked when planning an itinerary. In Philadelphia, after you've seen the Liberty Bell, walk a couple blocks to Old St. Joseph Church and make a visit to the Blessed Sacrament. In Chicago, take the architectural cruise along the shore of Lake Michigan; then on Sunday morning, go to one of the sung Masses at the St. John Cantius Church, where the music is sublime. And in San Antonio, Texas, after exploring the Alamo, head over to the St. Ferdinand Cathedral where the remains of the heroes of that desperate battle lie buried.

I hope this travel guide will convince you to include a Catholic site or two the next time you travel. I've visited more than a few of the sites in this book, but there are so many more I'd like to see. For you, this may be the starting point for a life-long interest in fascinating Catholic sites in America. For me, it's my Catholic bucket list.

ALABAMA

CULLMAN | Ave Maria Grotto, St. Bernard's Abbey
1600 St. Bernard Dr. SE • Cullman, AL 35055
256-734-4110 • www.avemariagrotto.com

When he was only fourteen years old, Michael Zoettl left his family in Bavaria in southern Germany to travel to the United States with Fr. Gamelbert Brunner and enter St. Bernard's Abbey in Alabama. After he concluded his studies, Michael made his vows as a Benedictine monk and took the name "Joseph." He was assigned to the menial tasks necessary to keep the monastery running, including shoveling coal for the abbey's power plant. Although Joseph was obedient to his superiors and did his best, he found the work tedious. For relief, in his spare time, he began to build miniature shrines that held little holy statues. These miniatures were sold at the abbey gift shop and the proceeds sent to the missions.

Soon, Brother Joseph had expanded into a new line of miniatures—building replicas of holy sites from around the world. Between 1932 and 1958—the year he retired—Brother Joseph created more than 125 little models of famous churches and sacred sites. But Brother Joseph also had a patriotic side— he designed minimemorials to fallen veterans of World War II, a tribute to the Statue of Liberty, and a replica of the Alamo. He also made a model of the abbey power plant that he knew so well.

As is true of folk art—and folk art was Brother Joseph's specialty—there is a naïve, whimsical charm to his creations. First, as a monk vowed to poverty, he had no money to buy materials for his miniatures; instead he relied on what he could find and what people gave him. Visitors to the Grotto will discover that Brother Joseph used concrete, ceramic tiles, and seashells, among other materials, for his little structures and embellished them with bits of costume jewelry, plastic animals, and marbles (the toy, not the stone). His models are not to scale, and often the perspective is off, but he can be forgiven—Brother Joseph never saw Jerusalem or St. Peter's Basilica in person, so he relied on postcards of these sites. Postcards rarely show the rear of a famous landmark, but rather than leave the back of his models blank, Joseph filled them in by imagining what they might look like.

The arrangement of the miniatures is also a bit offbeat. For example, located just above the replica of St. Peter's Basilica is the model of the Abbey of Monte Cassino, and to one side of St. Peter's is the replica of the Alamo.

To display Brother Joseph's ever-growing body of work, his brother monks set aside three wooded acres of the abbey grounds. Visitors still come to admire these quirky little creations, including Brother Joseph's final work, a model of the Lourdes Basilica, completed when he was eighty years old.

Before you head over to the gift shop, or back to your car, visit the abbey church and say a prayer for the repose of the soul of Brother Joseph, whose work has touched the hearts of so many pilgrims. Add another prayer for amateur artists and artisans who bring joy and inspiration into other people's lives.

For days and times when the Grotto and abbey are open to visitors, consult the website.

Irondale | Casa Maria Convent and Retreat House
3721 Belmont Rd. • Irondale, AL 35210
205-956-6760 • www.sisterservants.org

Irondale, Alabama, seems to attract a fair amount of holiness. It was here that Mother Angelica launched her round-the-clock cable network, Eternal Word Television Network (EWTN). She founded a new community of priests and brothers. And now, about a block and a half from EWTN's studios, is an order of women religious, the Sister Servants of the Eternal Word.

The nuns, most of them in their twenties and thirties, dress in ankle-length habits, wearing veils, and with St. Dominic's fifteen-decade rosary hanging from their belts. They follow a life that balances the active with the contemplative. Their work in the world is to teach the Catholic faith to children and adults, and to host religious retreats led by such renowned preachers and teachers as Fr. Mitch Pacwa, SJ, and Fr. Andrew Apostoli, CFR. There is a wide selection of retreats to choose from—for men, women, couples, mothers and daughters, as well as retreats that correspond with the liturgical year, such as a retreat to prepare for Lent, Holy Week, and the great solemnity of the resurrection at Easter.

The convent and retreat house are very attractive—a white-washed exterior with red tile roof, which gives the place a Spanish feel. The grounds are lovely—part landscaped garden beds, part untamed woodland where the sisters let nature be nature.

The sisters' schedule—and retreatants are welcome to join them in their chapel for all of these services—begins with a Holy Hour at 6 AM and concludes at "lights out" at 10 PM. Mass is offered daily. The sisters recite the Divine Mercy Chaplet daily, and they pray the rosary three times a day. The sisters cultivate among themselves and share with their visitors their great devotion to the Blessed Sacrament and love for the Blessed Virgin Mary, particularly under her title, Our Lady of Fatima. In addition, the sisters are committed to reviving the Church's treasury of great liturgical music.

Casa Maria is a growing community, and as tends to be the case with religious orders that are still new and growing, living space for the nuns is in short supply, and accommodations for guests is limited. If you would like to make a retreat at the convent, it is essential that you call well in advance. There is a suggested donation for retreats—please consult the Casa Maria website for details.

And during your retreat's downtime, take the short walk over to EWTN and see the place where Mother Angelica's Catholic cable empire began and is still going strong.

Casa Maria Convent and Retreat House is a place where you can revitalize your faith.

ALASKA

Juneau | Shrine of St. Thérèse
21425 Glacier Highway • Juneau, AK
907-586-2227 • www.shrineofsainttherese.org

In terms of settings, the Shrine of St. Thérèse may enjoy the finest view in the United States. It is located in the Tongass National Forest, overlooking an inlet of the Inside Passage. The shrine, including a stone chapel, crypt, and labyrinth, looks out on jagged, snow-
covered mountain peaks rising above the opposite shore. To walk the shrine's grounds is to be filled with wonder at the magnificence of God's creation.

The shrine was the brainchild of Fr. William G. LeVasseur, SJ. At a time when there was no Catholic retreat center in Alaska, Fr. LeVasseur intended this shrine to fill that void. Bishop Joseph Raphael Crimont, who served as vicar apostolic of all of Alaska, gave his permission for the project, and decided to dedicate it to St. Thérèse of Lisieux, who had just been canonized in 1925, The bishop had a deep devotion to Thérèse and was even acquainted with members of her family. Work on the beautiful stone chapel began in 1937.

To be honest, it is not easy to reach the shrine. It lies twenty-two miles outside Juneau, and there is no public transportation to it. Your only options are to rent a car (the best choice if you plan to make a retreat), rent a cab (the driver will charge by the hour), or join a tour via bus, but bear in mind that most tour groups rarely stay longer than thirty minutes.

Retreatants have a choice of accommodations: the Lodge, which sleeps twenty-four; the Jubilee Cabin, which sleeps fourteen; and, the lovely Little Flower Cabin, which sleeps four. There is also the one-room Hermitage cabin, which has no electricity or running water, so it is a much more ascetical experience than the Lodge and cabins.

In her brief life, St. Thérèse dedicated herself to contemplation and deepening her love for God. When you're visiting the island, ask her to intercede for you that God will grant you those gifts.

Open daily, weather permitting, 8:30 AM to 10:00 PM (April to September), 8:30 AM to 8:00 PM (October to March).

ARIZONA

Tucson | Redemptorist Renewal Center
7101 Picture Rocks Rd. • Tucson, AZ
520-744-3400 • www.desertrenewal.org

Set amid the arid but dramatic Sonoran Desert, the Redemptorist Fathers dedicated their church, appropriately, to Our Lady of the Desert. It is built low to the ground, with a wide arch that welcomes worshippers into the sanctuary. It is constructed of stone and large wooden beams, so the interior is austere but very handsome.

Third- and fourth-century Christians went into the desert of Egypt to find God in silence and solitude. That's what the Redemptorists offer at their retreat center. They welcome day visitors—as well as those who want to stay for a while—to restore their spiritual equilibrium (tough to do in this world, where there is so much noise and so many distractions). Check with the center in advance about availability of a room in the retreat house.

The Redemptorists offer Mass every morning. On Saturday, they pray the Novena to Our Lady of Perpetual Help, and they hear confessions and offer anointing of the sick. If you have never invoked the Mother of Perpetual Help, this is an excellent place to learn about her title, the meaning of her image, and the many graces that have been granted to those who have asked for her intercession.

Tucson | San Xavier del Bac Mission
1950 W. San Xavier Rd. • Tucson, AZ 85746
520-294-2624 • www.sanxaviermission.org

Since the 1500s, the American Southwest has been blessed with a bumper crop of missions. Of those that have survived the centuries, many are very beautiful, but in terms of aesthetics, it's hard to beat San Xavier del Bac Mission. The pure white towers of the mission church set against the endless blue sky of Arizona is an unforgettable sight. But the experience gets even better when you step through the exuberantly carved, three-story-tall, terra cotta–colored portal.

Fr. Eusebio Kino, a Jesuit missionary, established a mission here among the Tohono O'odham nation in 1692, but a host of circumstances prevented him from ever building a suitable church. The church you see today was begun in 1783 by Franciscan Father Juan Bautista Velderrain, who brought an architect up from Mexico, and hired a large number of O'odham craftsmen to construct a house of worship so lovely that it came to be called "The White Dove of the Missions."

The church interior is virtually unchanged from the late eighteenth century, when all these wonderful works of art, all of them dedicated to the greater glory of God, were installed. The paintings, sculptures, and other treasures you see inside the church were created by artists in Queretaro, Mexico. Prominent above the high altar is the sculpture of the mission's patron, St. Francis Xavier (1506–1552). The first missionary priest of the newly founded Society of Jesus (Jesuits), he spent his life planting the Catholic faith in India, the Moluccas, and Japan, where he converted and baptized thousands, perhaps tens of thousands.

Best of all, San Xavier is not some sterile historic site—it is a working, living parish where Mass is said daily, confessions are heard, and the Blessed Sacrament is exposed for public adoration. And there is a parish school. When you visit San Xavier, you are not a tourist, you are the welcome guest of a community of Native Americans, Latinos, and Anglos who have been worshipping together in this glorious church for more than two hundred years. Give yourself time not only to explore this mission, but to pray and meditate in this remarkable holy place on the dedication and sacrifice Fr. Kino and the countless other missionaries who planted the faith in the American Southwest.

Open daily from 7 AM to 5 PM, except during certain special religious services. For regular Mass times and schedule of special services, consult the website.

ARKANSAS

ALTUS | Church of St. Mary
5118 St. Mary's Lane • Altus, AR 72821
479-468-2585 • www.stmarysaltus.org

It's unusual to run into a church with three names. The parish calls itself—and just about everyone in Altus, Catholics and non-Catholics alike— "St. Mary's." But it has two more dedications: Our Lady of Perpetual Help and  Our Lady Help of Christians. No one seems to know why the dedication is under two titles of the Blessed Mother, but it's a safe bet that St. Mary's became the shorthand way to refer to the church.

When you think of large Catholic populations in the United States, Arkansas is probably not going to be the state that springs to mind. Yet, according to a study by the Glenmary Research Center (operated by the Glenmary Home Missioners), there are about 122,000 Catholics in Arkansas, which places them as a distant fourth among denominations in the state.

One of the glories of Catholic Arkansas is the Church of St. Mary. It makes an impression even before you step inside—built of golden sandstone in the Romanesque style, it crowns a hill on the outskirts of Altus.

Now that you've admired the exterior, it's time to experience the interior. The only word for the church decoration is "exuberant." There is color everywhere—glorious stained glass windows and decorative flourishes on the ceiling, the choir loft, and along the upper parts of the wall.

But the stars of the church are the painted Stations of the Cross and the powerful murals, which have reminded so many visitors of the dramatic murals Michelangelo painted on the Sistine Chapel ceiling. Are they masterpieces like Michelangelo's? No. But they are impressive nonetheless. And against this riot of color and sacred images is the wooden high altar and communion rail, stained a rich walnut. With so many things distracting the eye, the dark wooden altar and rail draw the worshippers' attention to what is most important in the church—the place where Mass is said and where the faithful receive Communion.

They don't build churches like this anymore. But at the end of the nineteenth century and the beginning of the twentieth, this style could be found across America. In the case of St. Mary's, the lavish decoration was a cultural necessity: the founders of the parish were Germans and German-speaking Swiss. This rich style was what they were used to in their homelands, and they recreated it in Arkansas.

Wander about the church slowly, and you'll encounter all manner of surprises. For example, the depiction of the Fifth Station in which Simon of Cyrene and a little boy, perhaps Simon's son, help Jesus carry the cross.

Once you've finished your tour, it's time to kneel down and pray. And as you do, remember the immigrants who sacrificed to build this glorious church, the priests—most of them Benedictine monks—who served the parishioners faithfully, and the artists who offered their best to God.

The church is open most days from 8:00 PM to 4:30 PM. Check the website to confirm that Mass is not being said at the time you would like to visit.

CALIFORNIA

CARMEL | Carmel Mission Basilica
3080 Rio Rd. • Carmel, CA 93923
831-624-1271 • www.carmelmission.org

The full name of this mission is San Carlos Borromeo del Rio Carmelo. St. Junipero Serra founded it in 1771. Of the nine missions Fr. Serra established in California, this was his favorite. He is buried here, and since his canonization, the mission church is home to his shrine.

The mission itself is glorious. The church is the focal point, of course, and it is hard to convey just how lovely it is. An arch of beautifully carved stone draws you through the main doors and into the church. To one side, rising above the entrance is a bell tower crowned by a unique dome, shaped like an oval cut in half. It's not unusual for there be a rose window above the main door of a Catholic church. But, at Carmel, instead of a rose, the window is in the shape of a starburst.

The church is filled with works of art imported from Spain, Mexico, and Italy. Naturally, the reredos, or altarpiece, grabs every visitor's attention. It stands thirty feet high and covers the entire sanctuary wall. At the center is a large crucifix with statues of the Blessed Virgin Mary and St. John the Evangelist standing beside Christ on the cross. Images of other saints, all of them painted in the vivid colors Spanish and Mexican artists favored, fill niches in the reredos.

Beside the church is a quadrangle, with lovely plantings. The mission church can be crowded, so the mission garden is a good place to retire and give yourself a little time for contemplation.

On September 23, 2015, during his visit to Washington, Pope Francis led a canonization ceremony and declared Fr. Serra a saint. A canonization is a joyful event, but in some quarters, controversy is swirling around Fr. Serra. Some Native American activists and their supporters charge Serra with flogging Native American converts who tried to leave the missions and with damaging the ecosystem of California by introducing European livestock that destroyed much of the plant-life and drove off the wild game the Native Americans depended on for food. Some see Serra as an agent of Spanish imperialism who abused the Native Americans he converted to the Catholic faith. Furthermore, Native Americans who became part of the mission system eventually lost their culture and even forgot their tribe's language.

But if Fr. Serra has detractors, he also has defenders who suggest that he was a man of his times, a missionary committed to his vocation and the Native Americans.

Carmel Mission is a lovely place to pray for all missionaries who leave their homes and sacrifice their lives to bring the Catholic faith and all the aid they can summon to people far away.

The mission often sponsors special events, and on weekends, there are many weddings. Check with the church office for the opening hours for the day of your visit.

DANVILLE | San Damiano Retreat Center
710 Highland Ave. • Danville, CA 94526
925-837-9141 • www.sandamiano.org

San Damiano is a classic: rounded arches, a shady cloister, and a red-tiled roof. The Franciscan friars operate the retreat center, and this style of architecture was perfected by the Spanish and Mexican Franciscan missionaries who were among the first Europeans to settle in California.

At the heart of the friary and retreat center is a large, enclosed cloister garden. The Franciscans have expanded their landscaping to include the grounds around San Damiano, and they've added an organic vegetable garden. Many retreatants help the friars maintain this beautiful place by serving as garden volunteers.

Aside from daily Mass and mealtimes, there is no schedule at San Damiano, such as you would find at a Trappist abbey. You can be as social or as solitary as you like. If you decide to strike up conversations with your fellow retreatants, the friars ask that you keep the volume of your voice down so as to preserve the peaceful atmosphere of San Damiano. And the friars are available for spiritual direction.

San Damiano offers a variety of activities and events that range from a regularly scheduled ecumenical prayer service, Stations of the Cross during Lent, lectures, workshops, and retreats. You'll find a calendar of events on the San Damiano website.

All the bedrooms include a private bath, and bed linens. The cost of a retreat begins at $100 for the first night at San Damiano, and $85 for every subsequent night. Meals are included. For times when the retreat center welcomes visitors, check the center website.

Los Angeles | Cathedral of Our Lady of the Angels
555 W Temple St. • Los Angeles, CA 90012
213-680-5200 • www.olacathedral.org

Drivers zooming along the Hollywood Freeway (that is, assuming that the notorious Los Angeles traffic isn't snarled) will see a stark, huge building of unusual architectural design. This is the Cathedral of Our Lady of the Angels, and it is unlike any other cathedral you have ever visited. It draws upon no classic architectural style, and it has a host of unconventional features. For example, there are virtually no right angles here.

While it cost the Archdiocese of Los Angeles $250 million to build, this is a church that not everyone will love. The bronze sculpture of Mary over the main door may strike some Catholics who have a deep devotion to Our Lady as a bit cold and unappealing. But for visitors whose taste in art runs toward the more traditional, there are twenty-five very beautiful tapestries depicting 135 saints and beatified persons. The portraits are incredibly lifelike.

Admirers of the cathedral describe it as "inspiring" and "awesome," and comment favorably on the many extra features of the site's more than five acres, including a vast plaza, a café, and a sculpture garden that is popular with children. After the quiet inside the church, the garden could be a good place to let the kids blow off steam.

Among the cathedral's eleven chapels is one dedicated to the Roman martyr, St. Vibiana. Her relics were found in the Roman catacombs in 1853 and given by Pope Pius IX to Bishop Thaddeus Amat. St. Vibiana was enshrined in Los Angeles' old cathedral in 1876.

Open Monday through Friday 6:30 AM to 6:00 PM; Saturday 9 AM to 6 PM; Sunday 7 AM to 6 PM. Concerts, special services, and other special events may disrupt the cathedral's schedule. A guided tour of the cathedral is available; call the tour coordinator at (213) 680-5215 to inquire about times of the tour and where to meet your guide.

COLORADO

San Luis | Stations of the Cross and La Capilla de Todos Los
Santos at Sangre de Cristo Parish
512 Church Pl. • San Luis, CO 81152
719-992-0122 • www.sdcparish.org

Set in an austere landscape, but
backed up by a spectacular view
of the snowcapped Rocky Mountains
is a shrine that captures the deep religious devotion of Hispanic Americans.
In 1990, a sculptor named Humberto
Maestas began a major project—fifteen life-size bronze sculptures
of the Stations of the Cross, the fourteen scenes of Christ's Passion
and death on the Cross. In a departure from tradition, Maestas
added a fifteenth sculpture of the risen Christ.

The sculptures are arranged along a trail that climbs an arid hill.
There is a bench in front of each one so that pilgrims can sit, pray,
and meditate on the suffering of Our Lord and the Blessed Mother.
The sculptures are beautifully detailed, and Maestas manages to
convey the raw human emotion in each scene. Perhaps the most
dramatic is of one of the executioners nailing Christ to the cross.
With his arm fully extended and a hammer in his hand, you can
imagine the agony of Jesus as the nail pierced his flesh and bone.

La Capilla de Todos Los Santos—the Chapel of All Saints—
crowns another hill. The chapel is small and rather plain, but
there are fine works of saints, done in the traditional folk art style
of this region. Following the Stations and praying in the chapel are

moving experiences. The parish is very active, and parish priests in the diocese organize parish pilgrimages to the shrine, but there are also other pilgrims who come from far distances to pray here.

Open Monday through Thursday, 8:30 AM to 4:00 PM.

Virginia Dale | Abbey of St. Walburga Retreat House
1029 Benedictine Way • Virginia Dale, CO 80536
970-472-0612 • www.walburga.org

A handful of German Benedictine nuns who were refugees from the Nazis founded this abbey in 1935. It is a thriving community. In fact, the sisters had to build a new monastery complex— they were receiving so many vocations that they had run out of room in the original abbey.

The style of the abbey blends the traditional with the contemporary, the best expression of which is the stunning abbey church. The architecture is a good reflection of the nuns, who wear the full traditional Benedictine habit but chant or pray the Divine Office in English. If you can arrange your schedule to visit the nuns on the eve or the evening of one of the solemnities of the church year or for an extended overnight stay, you'll hear the nuns chant the Divine Office using the traditional Gregorian plainsong.

The abbey is located in an isolated mountain valley about thirty-five miles north of Fort Collins. There is no Wi-Fi at St. Walburga, and because of its location on the valley floor, you won't get cell phone service either. So lock your devices in the trunk of your car and immerse yourself in the serenity of this place. You'll find it is easier to talk to God when you are free from the distractions of electronics.

You'll have a private bedroom with your own full bathroom. The suggested donation for each overnight stay is $65 per person. That includes three meals a day. If you are coming only for the day, with no overnight, the suggested donation is $20, and that includes lunch. The sisters also offer programs that range from a Gregorian chant workshop to classes on contemporary sacred art. And one of the nuns leads nature hikes. Reservations are required, and you must register for a retreat. You'll find the form on the abbey website, along with the hours the abbey is open and further information on retreats.

CONNECTICUT

BETHLEHEM | Abbey of Regina Laudis
273 Flanders Rd. • Bethlehem, CT 06751
203-266-7727 • www.abbeyofreginalaudis.org

Cloistered Benedictine nuns do not do a lot of television, but one of the nuns at the Abbey of Regina Laudis continually draws camera crews to this abbey in a semirural town. In the late 1950s and early 1960s, Mother Dolores, prioress of the abbey, was a rising Hollywood starlet playing opposite such leading men as Montgomery Clift, George Hamilton, Stephen Boyd, and most famously, Elvis, in *Loving You* and *King Creole*. Several of Mother Dolores's friends from her days on the big screen were generous benefactors of the abbey, including Grace Kelly, Paul Newman, and Patricia Neal. The film, *Come to the Stable*, starring Loretta Young and Celeste Holm, is loosely based on the founding of the abbey in the late 1940s.

The abbey occupies 450 acres of dense woods and carefully maintained farmland, including vegetable gardens, apple orchards, hay fields, and pastures for the abbey's cattle and sheep. The architectural jewel of this hardworking abbey is the Church of Jesu Fili Mariae—Jesus, Son of Mary. Several of the nuns and a Jesuit priest trained as an architect contributed to the design of the church, which is inspired by traditional New England architecture modified for the needs of a monastic community.

All the windows are clear so that natural light pours into the church even on overcast days. A tall iron grill, handcrafted in the abbey's forge, separates the nuns from the congregation. To the right of the altar is a freestanding, rough-hewn column of granite that holds the tabernacle. Here the nuns meet seven times a day for the Divine Office and to celebrate Mass. All of the music is traditional Gregorian chant sung in Latin. To hear the nuns ethereal chanting is to immerse yourself in a form of music that has nurtured the Catholic Church for 1,500 years.

One of the abbey's treasures is an elaborate crèche, or Nativity scene, created in Naples, Italy, about 1720 as a gift for King Victor Amadeus II. The sixty human figures, twenty animal figures, as well as the intricate architectural background are back on display after a four-year restoration project. You'll find the crèche in the eighteenth-century Bellamy Barn.

Women and men are welcome to make a retreat at Regina Laudis. Accommodations for women are at St. Gregory's guesthouse, men at St. Joseph's guesthouse. Meals are served in the refectory, or dining room, of each guesthouse, and each house also has its own common room where retreatants can socialize. All guests are encouraged to spend some time in a private meeting with the abbey's guest mistress. Reservations must be made in writing via postal mail. There is also the Abbey art shop.

If you are not especially familiar with Gregorian chant, hearing the nuns sing the Divine Office several times a day will make you a devotee of this ancient, ethereal music, which is one of the greatest treasures of the Catholic Church.

The Church of Jesu Fili Mariae is open during the day from 8 AM until after Compline at 7:30 PM. The Creche is open daily from Easter through autumn from 10 AM to 4 PM. It is closed during winter and reopens at Easter.

DARIEN | Convent of St. Birgitta and Vikingsborg Guest House
4 Runkenhage Rd. • Darien, CT 06820
203-655-1068 • www.birgittines-us.com

If you have never heard of the Bridgettine or Birgittine nuns and monks, don't be too hard on yourself. This religious order, founded by St. Bridget or Birgitta of Sweden in 1370, all but died out during the Protestant Reformation, when the community's convents and abbeys in northern Europe (the home turf of the Bridgettines) were destroyed and the monks and nuns scattered. In 1535, after Henry VIII's break with Rome, St. Richard Reynolds, a Bridgettine monk from England's renowned Syon Abbey, was among the first five Catholic clergymen to be martyred by the king.

In 1911, the Bridgettine order was revived by Blessed Elisabetta Hesselblad, a Swede who had emigrated to the United States. Although raised a Lutheran, she had converted to the Catholic faith and then accepted her vocation to be a nun of the nearly extinct Bridgettine order. Her convent in Darien, Connecticut, is the only house of the Bridgettine nuns in the United States, but thanks to Mother Elisabetta, Bridgettine houses can be found across Europe, as well as in India and Mexico.

The Bridgettines are semi-contemplatives, who spend a good part of their day in prayer and meditation, but also take on whatever work the local bishop asks of them, from teaching catechism classes to children to caring for the elderly. From their founding, the nuns have offered hospitality to guests who are looking for a temporary retreat from the noise and troubles of the secular world, and the sisters continue that tradition at their retreat house, Vikingsborg.

The house, which overlooks the Long Island Sound, is a late nineteenth-century stone mansion given to the nuns in 1957 by a well-to-do benefactor. Vikingsborg is located in Darien, one of the wealthiest and loveliest towns in Connecticut. The sisters welcome men and women, singles, couples, families, and groups. Accommodations are limited, so if you would like to make a retreat at Vikingsborg, it is essential to contact the center well in advance. The sisters ask for $110 per day, per guest, to cover their expenses. This rate includes a room with a private or shared bath (your choice), and three full meals a day.

Vikingsborg has a library, a meeting room, and a recreation room that contains the convent's only television—although, given the peace and beauty of the walking trails, gardens, and views of the Sound, guests rarely turn it on.

The convent chapel is charming; both the nuns and the guests worship here together. The Bridgettines' cycle of daily prayer begins early in the morning and concludes in the evening. Mass is celebrated each day in the chapel, and the nuns gather in the late afternoon to pray the rosary. Several days a week, the Blessed Sacrament is exposed in the chapel for public veneration. Guests are welcome at all of these services.

Ecumenical outreach is another of the nuns' apostolates, and so they welcome visitors of all faiths or no faith. One of their earliest supporters was a Protestant neighbor, Anne Morrow Lindbergh, wife of aviator Charles Lindbergh. Her house stood near the convent, and when hearing the convent's bell, Mrs. Lindbergh is known to have joined the nuns, briefly, in prayer. When you're at the convent, imitate Mrs. Lindbergh.

NEW HAVEN | Knights of Columbus Museum
One State St. • New Haven, CT 06511
203-865-0400 • www.kofcmuseum.org

Why New Haven? Because that's where, in 1882, young Fr. Michael J. McGivney founded the Knights. Remember that in the nineteenth century, America was teeming with immigrants. In 1882, it was a great wave of Italians and Slavs who came ashore and went looking for jobs in the cities. Fr. McGivney saw a desperate need among widows and orphans, so the Knights took up the task of being a mutual-aid society.

With anti-Catholicism rampant in the United States, the Knights worked to keep young Catholics away from organizations that might lure them away from their faith. In fact, loyalty to the Catholic faith and to America's unshakable devotion to liberty has been—and still is—the bedrock on which the Knights were founded.

The Knights built the museum to celebrate their centennial. It is a starkly modern, even abstract building. And it is filled with wonderful things, including the chalice and paten used by James Augustine Healy (1830–1890). He is remembered as Catholic America's first black bishop, although he considered himself to be white (his father was an Irishman). Then there is Christopher Columbus memorabilia and even the cross that stood for nearly four hundred years over the main entrance to St. Peter's Basilica.

If you live anywhere within striking distance of New Haven, come to the museum at Christmastime, when the curators bring out their collection of seventy-six Nativity scenes. One is more beautiful than the next.

And here are two more reasons to visit: admission to the museum is free, and parking in the museum's lot is also free—a real blessing in a city where parking is at a premium.

The museum is open daily from 10 AM until 5 PM. It is closed on Thanksgiving, Christmas Eve, Christmas Day, and Good Friday.

DELAWARE

Wilmington | **St. Anthony of Padua Church**
1715 West Ninth St. • Wilmington, DE 19805
302-421-3700 • www.stanthonynet.org

If you watched the broadcast of the funeral Mass of Beau Biden, the son of Vice President Joe Biden, then you saw the lovely Church of St. Anthony. This is the parish of Beau and his family.

If you are at all familiar with Italian Catholic culture, then you won't be surprised to learn that St. Anthony's stands in the heart of Wilmington's Little Italy neighborhood. Along with the Blessed Mother and St. Joseph, St. Anthony of Padua is one of the most popular saints among Italians (in spite of the fact that Anthony was not Italian—he was from Portugal).

The church was built in the Romanesque style and modeled on the Basilica of San Zeno in Verona, Italy. The exterior is grand, and the interior is gorgeous. Everywhere there are rounded arches supported by colored marble columns, a motif the Romanesque architects picked up from Byzantine architects who erected magnificent churches throughout the Roman Empire in the late fourth and early fifth centuries. Around the walls are roundels of the saints, and covering the vaulted ceiling over the main altar are beautiful mosaics.

If you are traveling through Delaware in mid-June, you may be in time for the parish's annual Italian Festival, celebrated around

June 13, the feast day of St. Anthony. In addition to homemade Italian specialties made by members of the parish, there is also a competition among home winemakers.

Many American Catholics believe that the old ethnic parishes are a thing of the past, but at St. Anthony's, parishioners take great pride in the parish's Italian heritage and go the extra mile to celebrate and preserve it.

Consult the parish website for Mass times, and contact the parish office to learn when the church is open to visitors.

East Room of the White House
1600 Pennsylvania Ave. • Washington, DC 20500
202-456-7041 • www.whitehouse.gov

The East Room is one of the original rooms of the White House, designed by architect James Hoban (an Irish Catholic). Over the centuries, it has served a variety of purposes, including as a setting for state dinners, for concerts, and for awards ceremonies. It has also been the site of one-of-a-kind moments in American history: John F. Kennedy lay in state here after his assassination, and it was here that Richard Nixon announced to his staff that he was resigning the presidency.

During the presidency of Andrew Jackson, two other historic events took place here that Catholics will find especially significant. In 1832, Jackson's ward, Mary Ann Lewis, was united in marriage to Joseph Pageot, a French diplomat; Fr. William Matthews of St. Patrick's Church presided. The Lewis-Pageot wedding was the first Catholic ceremony held in the White House, which was a daring decision on Jackson's part, given anti-Catholic sentiment in America at the time.

A year later Fr. Matthews returned to the White House to officiate at another sacrament—the baptism of the Pageots' first child. They named the baby boy Andrew Jackson Pageot. According to an account by Julia Ward Stickley in a July 1965 *Catholic Historical Review* article, "Catholic Ceremonies in the White House,

1832–1833," when Fr. Matthews asked the child's godparents the ritual question on behalf of the child, "Andrew Jackson, do you renounce Satan?" the president, thinking the priest was speaking to him, declared in a loud voice, "I do, most indubitably!"

By the way, while you're in the East Room, don't miss the full-length portrait of George Washington. It is the work of Gilbert Stuart, one of the most gifted portrait artists of late eighteenth- and early nineteenth-century America.

In 1814, as a British army of four thousand veteran troops bore down on Washington, First Lady Dolley Madison prepared to flee. Among the items she grabbed at the last minute was a copy of the Declaration of Independence and the Stuart portrait of Washington. The portrait of Martha Washington that hangs in the East Room was not in danger because it had not yet been painted—Martha's portrait dates from 1878.

In order to tour The White House and see the East Room, you must make a request to your member of Congress. Every visitor age eighteen and over must show a government-issued photo ID, such as a driver's license. Bear in mind that tours are limited to the morning hours, so it is necessary to make your reservation months in advance.

Nuns of the Battlefield Monument
1745 M Street NW
(where Rhode Island Avenue NW converges)
Washington, DC 20036

More than six hundred sisters nursed the wounded of the North and South during the Civil War. Sisters of a dozen religious orders, including the Ursulines, the Sisters of St. Joseph, the Sisters of the Holy Cross, and the Sisters of Mercy, worked in the hospitals during the war, but Mother Seton's Daughters of Charity supplied the largest number of nurses—270 sisters.

The Daughters of Charity are especially remembered for their work after the Battle of Gettysburg in 1863—their motherhouse is only fifteen miles from Gettysburg. The day after the battle, on the Fourth of July, the first Daughters of Charity arrived. They found fifty thousand wounded men, many of them still lying on the battlefield. Sister Petronilla Breen, Sister Juliana Chatard, and Sister Emerito Quinlan went immediately to the battlefield, where they cleaned and bandaged soldiers' wounds, administered pain-killers, and prayed with the dying. In the days that followed, more sisters from Emmitsburg came to Gettysburg, where they were assigned to the hospital in the Methodist Church and the hospital in the Catholic Church of St. Francis Xavier. The wounded filled every pew in St. Francis—in the nave and the gallery—and they lay side by side on the floor, even inside the sanctuary. The church vestibule was used for surgery.

Most orders of nuns in the United States in the mid-nineteenth century operated hospitals, and as a result, many of the sisters had medical training (unlike most of the laywomen who volunteered as nurses).

According to *Nuns of the Battlefield*, by historian Ellen Ryan Jolly (Kessinger Publishing, 2010), military surgeons and civilian doctors came to prefer the nursing nuns to laywomen nurses. In addition to their medical skills, the nuns acquired a reputation of being patient, efficient, and tireless, following doctors' orders, not being argumentative, and not complaining about their accommodations (although they did insist upon a room that would serve as their chapel).

In contrast, many physicians complained that laywomen nurses were quarrelsome, defiant, and dissatisfied. Worst of all were the nurses who formed romantic attachments with their patients— something that was not generally an issue with the nuns. The federal government discovered yet another quality that made the nuns superior—laywomen demanded a salary of $12 per month, but the nuns worked for free.

A monument to these selfless women was commissioned from Irish sculptor Jerome Connor in 1924 by the Ladies Auxiliary of the Ancient Order of Hibernians. Conner created a dignified tribute to these heroic women who worked tirelessly to ease the suffering, save the lives, and perhaps even save the souls of the men they nursed. But after he had completed the sculpture, the Hibernians were slow to pay Conner—so he sued them.

On view seven days a week, twenty-four hours a day, year-round.

Cathedral of St. Matthew the Apostle
1725 Rhode Island Ave. NW • Washington, DC 20036
202-347-3215 • www.stmatthewscathedral.org

Directly across the street from the Nuns of the Battlefield Monument is Washington, DC's Catholic cathedral. While the parish dates back to 1840, the current grand red-brick church was not begun until 1893. The interior is rich in newly cleaned and refurbished mosaics and other works of art.

In November 1963, the cathedral was the location of the

requiem Mass for President John F. Kennedy. A marble plaque set in the floor before the gates of the sanctuary marks the spot where the casket of the assassinated president rested during the funeral. Guided tours of the cathedral are available, but contact the parish office to make a reservation.

Open Sunday through Friday, 6:30 AM to 6:30 PM, Saturday 7:30 AM to 6:30 PM, on federal holidays 7:30 AM to 1:00 PM.

St. Augustine's Church
15th and V streets, NW • Washington, DC 20009
202-265-1470 • www.saintaugustine-dc.org

On New Year's Day 1889, Daniel Rudd, a zealous Catholic and former slave from Kentucky, opened the first Black Lay Catholic Congress at St. Augustine, a parish that served the African American Catholic community in the nation's capital. Rudd believed that in post–Civil War America the Catholic Church could help African Americans enter mainstream society. At his invitation, eighty-five black Catholic laymen assembled at St. Augustine's to discuss ways to strengthen the unity of black Catholics and bring more African Americans to the faith.

Rudd and his fellow African American colleagues were bold when they confronted priests, bishops, and archbishops, asserting they had the same rights as white Catholics, and they wanted to clergy to recognize them. This was daring talk at a time when very few white people believed that blacks were their equal.

In Washington, St. Augustine's became the mother church for the city's black Catholics. It thrived, and the parish and its school are still thriving. Visit the church—it is beautiful in that old fashioned way. And keep an eye out for a one-of-a-kind stained glass window depicting St. Augustine and his mother, St. Monica, as dark-skinned Africans.

And if you can arrange it, go to Sunday Mass at St. Augustine's. At the 10 AM Mass, the parish's choir sings traditional hymns and great classical music. At the Gospel Mass the choir and band rock the house with spirituals and contemporary gospel music.

Contact the parish office in advance to find out when the church is open.

FLORIDA

Miami | National Shrine of Our Lady of Charity
3609 South Miami Ave. • Miami, FL 33133
305-854-2404 • www.ermitadelacaridad.org

After the 1959 Cuban revolution, the United States saw an enormous influx of refugees from Cuba in the wake of the Communist government taking over their nation. Many of them settled in Florida, particularly in the city of Miami.

It seemed natural that a replica of the statue of Our Lady of Charity, the national patron of the Cuban people, should be enshrined in Miami. After all, it was in Miami in 1961 that the Feast of Our Lady of Charity was first celebrated by Archbishop Coleman F. Carroll, who led thirty thousand Cuban exiles in prayer and a grand procession that carried the sacred image of the Blessed Mother—a replica of the original statue, newly arrived in Miami from Cuba—through the streets of the city.

The shrine church is starkly modern, crowned by a conical dome. It stands overlooking the Atlantic Ocean on land donated by Archbishop Carroll. Inside, over the main altar, is a large, dramatic mural that depicts Cuban patriots—clergy, religious, and laypeople—as well as scenes from Cuban history, including a touching depiction of a Cuban refugee family fleeing their homes in a small row boat to find safety and freedom in America.

Standing before the mural is the statue of Our Lady of Charity, beautifully dressed in elaborately embroidered robes.

The shrine is a busy place, with pilgrims flocking to the church daily for Mass, confession, or private devotions. In addition, based at the shrine, there is a chapter of the Confraternity of Our Lady of Charity, which was first founded in Cuba in the late 1600s. Members have an active outreach program to Catholics who have fallen away from their faith, they contribute to the support of the shrine, and they help organize the annual pilgrimages in honor of Our Lady.

Consult the shrine's bilingual website or contact the office for days and times when the shrine is open to visitors.

**St. Augustine | Mission Nombre de Dios and Shrine of
Our Lady of La Leche**
27 Ocean Ave. • St. Augustine, FL 32084
800-342-6529 • www.missionandshrine.org

The day was September 8, 1565, the Feast of the Nativity of the Blessed Virgin Mary, when Pedro Menéndez de Avilés, the leader of a party of Spanish colonists, came ashore at what is now St. Augustine, Florida.

His mission was twofold: to establish a colony for Spain in Florida and to begin the evangelization of the Native American tribes. Once ashore, Menéndez de Avilés knelt and kissed a wooden cross presented to him by Fr. Francisco López de Mendoza Grajales, one of four secular priests sent along as chaplains and missionaries. After this brief ceremony, Fr. Mendoza Grajales vested and celebrated the first Mass in what would become the United States. And so began the first permanent European settlement and the first Catholic mission in America. The mission was consecrated to Nombre de Dios—the Name of God.

That's a lot of firsts, and all these memorable events in America's Catholic history are commemorated today at the mission by a soaring cross that overlooks Matanzas Bay, a dramatic statue of Fr. Mendoza Grajales, and a rustic outdoor altar that recalls the improvised altar erected for the first Mass.

Early in the 1600s, the residents of the colony built a small chapel and installed over the altar a statue of Nuestra Señora de La Leche y Buen Parto—Our Lady of the Milk and of Happy Delivery. It was the first shrine to the Mother of God in America.

Devotion to Mary under this title may go back to the fourth century; certainly it was well-established in Bethlehem by the time the Crusaders arrived late in the eleventh century, and the statue had its own little chapel, the Milk Chapel, in the lower level of the Church of the Nativity. It was probably Crusaders who brought this devotion back to Europe, where it was especially popular in Spain.

War and bad weather took their toll on successive chapels of La Leche; the current chapel dates from 1875, and even it had to be restored after a hurricane swept through St. Augustine in 1914. The exterior is very attractive, with a stepped gable facade that gives the shrine an old-world look. The interior is austere—the Florida colony would never be the windfall Spain got in Mexico and Peru. But the simple decor draws the pilgrim's focus to exactly where it should be—to the large, beautifully painted wood sculpture of the Blessed Virgin nursing the infant Jesus.

The mission grounds are lovely, shaded by ancient trees and overlooking the bay. The Prince of Peace Church, built in 1965 to commemorate the 400th anniversary of the founding of the colony, is starkly modern and may not appeal to everyone. Mass is rarely celebrated in the church, but the Blessed Sacrament is exposed for public veneration during weekdays.

Visitors who prefer something more historic will enjoy a walk through the centuries-old cemetery and to the archaeological excavations of the original settlement and the Seloy Indian village.

Artifacts uncovered during the dig are displayed at the site's museum, along with antique sacred vessels and vestments on loan from the archives of the Diocese of St. Augustine.

Sarasota | The John and Mabel Ringling Museum of Art
5401 Bay Shore Rd. • Sarasota, FL 34243
941-359-5700 • www.ringling.org/museum-art

It is unexpected that a name associated with circus extravaganzas would also be the benefactor of a splendid art museum that displays one of the treasures of Catholic art—four Massive oil paintings by Peter Paul Rubens in praise of the Blessed Sacrament.

Circus acts made John Ringling a fortune, and like so many wealthy Americans of the late nineteenth and early twentieth centuries, he spent part of his fortune on collecting exquisite works of art to decorate his home and eventually to form the nucleus of a museum of fine art. In the 1920s, he purchased four very large oil paintings by Peter Paul Rubens from the Duke of Westminster, whose family had owned the masterpieces for more than a century.

The paintings were the first step of an ambitious commission Rubens accepted in 1625 from the Spanish princess, Clara, for a series of twenty tapestries for a convent of Poor Clare nuns, all of whose members were members of the Spanish royal family. The series of tapestries, known as "The Triumph of the Eucharist," were based on Rubens' glorious paintings—known as "cartoons" at the time, although there is nothing cartoonish, as we understand the term, about them.

The paintings are displayed in a grand gallery, the very first one a visitor sees on entering the Ringling Museum. They show Rubens at his best, with a lot of dramatic movement, swirling draperies, and vivid colors, especially bright red, which Rubens loved. The finished paintings were sent to a professional weaver who created the tapestries for the nuns. As fine as the tapestries are, in terms of color, they pale in comparison to Rubens's "cartoons."

The four paintings in the Ringling collection depict: the meeting of Abraham and the priest Melchizedek, who offered the patriarch bread and wine; the Israelites collecting manna, the bread that dropped down from Heaven, a gift from God to feed His people; a group portrait of the four evangelists—Matthew, Mark, Luke, and John; and a procession of saints who were devoted to and champions of the real presence of Christ in the Blessed Sacrament. In the procession, St. Clare of Assisi carries a monstrance containing the sacred host.

Rubens' paintings are glorious, and it is our privilege that they are here in the United States. But there is more going on in these paintings than you might suspect. According the website of the Prado Museum in Spain, which displays one of the paintings, Princess Isabel Clara Eugenia wanted the cartoons/tapestries to proclaim the doctrine of the real presence at a time when the Protestant churches insisted that the bread and wine were only symbols, that they were not the true body and blood, soul and divinity of Jesus Christ. Understanding that, these treasures become more than glorious works of art; they are an eloquent defense of one of the central doctrines of the Catholic faith. If you go to see these paintings, don't just admire their beauty and Rubens's skill, but let yourself be moved—as Princess Clara intended—to renew your love for Christ in the Blessed Sacrament.

The museum is open daily 10 AM to 5 PM, Thursday until 8 PM. It is closed on Thanksgiving, Christmas, and New Year's Day. Admission is free on Mondays. For other admission information, or to arrange a guided tour led by one of the museum's docents, please call, or consult the museum's website.

GEORGIA

ANDERSONVILLE | Andersonville National Historic Site
National Prisoner of War Museum
496 Cemetery Rd. • Andersonville, GA 31711
229-924-0343 • www.nps.gov/ande/index.htm

The Civil War prisoner of war camp here is among the most notorious in American history. About forty-five thousand Union prisoners were crowded into a large open pen. With no shelter, starvation rations, and contaminated  water, the prisoners barely clung to life. Some thirteen thousand died, most of them from malnutrition, scurvy, and dysentery.

By 1864, when the prison camp opened, it was hard enough for Confederate soldiers and civilians to find medical supplies and get enough to eat. As a result, there was very little left over for Union troops taken captive on the battlefield. The problem was made worse after the Union government abolished its prisoner-exchange program.

In 1864, Jean-Pierre Verot, the first Catholic bishop of St. Augustine, Florida, traveled to Georgia. At one point, his hosts took him to Andersonville. Although he was a champion of Southern independence, the sight of tens of thousands of sick, starving, dying men horrified him. Bishop Verot sent five priests to Andersonville to do whatever they could to bring spiritual comfort, as well as food and clean water, to the prisoners. It was a hopeless task, yet his self-sacrificing priests had this distinction: they were the only clergymen to minister to the prisoners of Andersonville.

Today Andersonville is a national historic site. A portion of the original stockade has been reconstructed, and there is a Prisoner of War Museum that tells the stories of POWs in all of America's military conflicts. A 26.5-acre site has been set aside as a cemetery for the dead of Andersonville. Of the 13,714 graves marked here, 921 are marked "Unknown." During your visit, remember to pray for the souls of the men who suffered and died in Andersonville, as well as for the five priests and Bishop Verot who sought to help these helpless men.

The park is open daily from 9:00 AM to 4:30 PM. It is closed on Thanksgiving, Christmas, and New Year's Day.

MILLEDGEVILLE | Andalusia Farm
2628 N. Columbia St. • Milledgeville, GA 31061
478-454-4029 • www.andalusiafarm.org

Andalusia Farm had belonged to the maternal grandfather of noted southern Catholic writer Flannery O'Connor. In his will, he left the place to his daughter, Regina (O'Connor's mother), and his brother, Louis. Regina managed the place, raising dairy cows and then beef cattle. Louis, who was well-off, supplied the farm equipment and took care of other major expenditures while Regina turned the five-hundred-acre farm about one hundred miles east of Atlanta into a prosperous business.

Flannery O'Connor had visited the place since childhood. As an adult, she lived for a time in New York City, and then spent a year living with the poet Robert Fitzgerald and his wife, Sally, in their home in Ridgefield, Connecticut. After she was diagnosed with lupus, she moved in with her mother at Andalusia.

In spite of her illness, O'Connor continued to write—short stories, novels, essays—and traveled from time to time to give lectures. Among her topics were the ties between religious faith and literature. Back at the farm, O'Connor amused herself by raising peacocks. Mother and daughter attended Mass at Sacred Heart Church, about four miles away in the little town of Milledgeville.

Andalusia Farm was O'Connor's home for the last thirteen years of her life. She died here in 1964, at the age of thirty-nine.

SAVANNAH | Flannery O'Connor Childhood Home
207 East Charlton St. • Savannah, GA 31401
912-233-6014 • www.flanneryoconnorhome.org

After seeing the site where Flannery O'Connor lived the last years of her life, travel about 160 miles east to her first home.

The noted Catholic author once explained why she liked to populate her short stories and novels with oddballs. The website of the Flannery O'Connor Childhood Home quotes her as saying, "Whenever I'm asked why Southern writers particularly have a penchant for writing about freaks, I say it is because we are still able to recognize one."

When readers speak about O'Connor, they tend to recall the hold her strange stories have on them, or her sharp, dry wit. What is rarely mentioned is that, in addition to being a gifted author (she won the O. Henry Award for short fiction three times), Flannery

O'Connor was also a devout Catholic. And from time to time O'Connor used her sly, ingenious sense of humor to defend her Catholic faith. *In The Habit of Being: Letters of Flannery O'Connor* (Farrar, Straus and Giroux, 1988), the author tells how on one occasion she was at a house party given for writers and other intellectuals. Somehow, the conversation turned to the Eucharist. One of the guests was Mary McCarthy, an author and lapsed Catholic, who said that she regarded the Blessed Sacrament as just a symbol. O'Connor replied, "Well, if it's symbol, to hell with it."

She was baptized Mary Flannery, perhaps because she was born on March 25, the Feast of the Annunciation. The place of her baptism was the Cathedral of St. John the Baptist, just across Lafayette Square from her family's home. According the website of the Flannery O'Connor Childhood Home, her family called her Mary; Flannery was the name she used in adulthood. She described herself as a "pigeon-toed child with a receding chin and a you-leave-me-alone-or-I'll-bite-you complex."

While other historic homes tend to be prettified, the staff of the O'Connor house have restored it to the way it appeared during the 1930s, the decade of the Depression, and the period when O'Connor's father, Edward, was diagnosed with lupus, an illness which took his life in 1941, when O'Connor was fifteen years old.

The O'Connor family lived here quietly. It would be as a young woman and an adult that Mary Flannery O'Connor developed the sharp tongue and weakness for grotesque characters that probably shocked her neighbors.

Open Friday through Wednesday, 1 PM to 4 PM. Closed on major holidays.

HONOLULU | Cathedral Basilica of Our Lady of Peace
1184 Bishop St. • Honolulu, HI 96813
808-536-7036 • www.cathedralofourladyofpeace.com

The exterior of this cathedral is very plain, even austere. But step inside and you'll discover a beautiful church with a fine white marble high altar, lovingly carved statues, stained glass windows designed by local artists,  galleries that on Sundays and holy days are filled with worshippers, and near the altar, two small shrines that hold a relic of St. Damien of Molokai, who was ordained at the cathedral in 1864, and the remains of St. Marianne Cope. The cathedral was built using materials native to Hawaii—coral blocks for the walls, and koa wood for the wainscoting and the doors.

In 2016 the cathedral was undergoing an extensive renovation to restore as much as possible its nineteenth-century appearance, including returning the pews to their original position facing the altar. In addition, a reliquary chapel will be constructed to enshrine the relics of St. Damien and St. Marianne. During a renovation project balancing the needs of the construction crew and the natural desire of Catholics to pray in a lovely historic church can be tricky.

Before you make the effort to visit Our Lady of Peace, call the cathedral office to learn the hours and location of Masses, and when the cathedral is open to visitors. If you have a few dollars to spare, consider making a contribution to the ambitious restoration fund—parishioners of Our Lady of Peace hope everything will be complete in time for the cathedral's 175th anniversary in 2018.

Molokai | St. Damien and St. Marianne Cope Sites
Kalaupapa National Historic Site • Kalaupapa Peninsula
Molokai, Hawaii 96742 • www.nps.gov/kala

In terms of landscapes and seascapes, Kalaupapa Peninsula on the island of Molokai is a glorious place. On three sides, there are wonderful vistas of the Pacific Ocean, and at the edge of the peninsula, rise sea cliffs almost four thousand feet high, the highest in the world, according to the *Guinness Book of World Records*.

As magnificent as Kalaupapa is, in the nineteenth century, this was a place of exile for lepers, known today as victims of Hansen's disease. Here the sick and the dying were dropped off by boats from the other Hawaiian Islands, while those majestic cliffs ensured that they could not escape their banishment and reach other parts of Molokai.

Over the decades, clergy from the Congregational and Mormon churches, Catholic priests, and sometimes, family and friends of the exiles came here to care for the sick and the dying. In 1873, Fr. Damien de Veuster, a priest from Belgium, volunteered to work at what was then known as "the leper colony." For the next sixteen years, Fr. Damien tended to the physical and spiritual health of his congregation, helping them build little houses rather than the shacks and lean-tos where so many of the victims lived, and restoring and expanding the Church of St. Philomena, dedicated to one of his favorite saints.

In 1888, Fr. Damien himself was dying from Hansen's Disease. He got in touch with Mother Marianne Cope, a Sister of St. Francis from Syracuse, New York, who had been trained in medicine. Fr. Damien asked Mother Marianne to come to Molokai with some of her sisters and care for the sick. The nuns came, and their first patient was Fr. Damien. In spite of the sisters' excellent care, Fr. Damien died in 1889, a few months after their arrival.

In addition to nursing the sick, Mother Marianne and her companions took over the operation of the Kalaupapa orphanages that gave a home to boys and girls who had lost their parents or had been abandoned. In 1918, Mother Marianne died here.

Both Fr. Damien and Mother Marianne were buried at Kalaupapa, the priest in the St. Philomena churchyard and Mother Marianne on the grounds of the Bishop Home for Girls. When the restoration of Honolulu's Cathedral Basilica Our Lady of Peace is complete, the relics of St. Damien and St. Marianne will be placed together in a chapel specially constructed to receive them.

The historic sites at Kalaupapa include the Church of St. Philomena, the parish of St. Damien, St. Marianne, and their patients. The interior of the church has been lovingly restored. Among the statues of the saints is one, naturally, of St. Damien in the habit of his religious order, the Society of the Sacred Hearts of Jesus and Mary. His grave can be found in the churchyard. St. Marianne's grave is on the grounds of the Bishop Home. Her monument is a sculpture of Christ leaning down from the Cross to embrace St. Francis of Assisi.

For information on how to reach Kalaupapa and to schedule a tour of the sacred and historic sites, call Damien Tours, 808-567-6171. For information about the historical site itself, contact the National Park Service through the website.

IDAHO

CATALDO | Coeur d'Alene's Old Mission State Park
Exit 39 I-90 • Coeur d'Alene, ID
208-682-3814
www.parksandrecreation.idaho.gov/parks/
coeur-d-alenes-old-mission

How the faith is first planted and then thrives in a particular region can be mysterious, and that's certainly the case with the establishment of the Catholic Church in Idaho. The Native American tribes first heard the basics  of the faith from an unlikely source—the rough, rugged French Canadian fur trappers and mountain men who traded with the Native Americans.

Early in the 1800s, nineteen Iroquois Catholics from the mission of Caughnawaga on the St. Lawrence River traveled west, settling eventually with the Flathead tribe. The leader of this band of Iroquois was a Catholic named Old Ignace, who piqued the interest of the Flatheads in Catholicism. But Ignace insisted that they needed the Black Robes, a common Native American term for Jesuit priests, to show them the way to heaven.

In the 1830s, three times delegations of Flatheads and their neighbors the Nez Perce traveled to St. Louis to ask for a Black Robe to come back with them to Idaho. Finally, in 1840, the bishop of St. Louis sent Fr. Pierre Jean De Smet, SJ, to evangelize the tribes who lived in the Rocky Mountains. Soon, more missionary priests arrived in the region, and two of them built a very humble mission church—the first Catholic church in Idaho, dedicated to the Sacred Heart—among the Coeur d'Alene tribe.

In 1850, a Jesuit from Italy, Fr. Antonio Ravalli, came to Sacred Heart and decided to build a more substantial church. Fr. Ravalli designed it in the Renaissance style of the churches he grew up among back in Italy, and members of his Coeur d'Alene congregation helped him build it.

When you enter the church, you'll see that the decor is unlike anything you would see in Italy. The walls are covered with printed cloth purchased from the Hudson's Bay Company. Someone donated rolls of blank newsprint, and Fr. Ravalli had Native American artists paint them and mount them to further adorn the church. Native American artisans also carved two of the holy statues for the church. And for lighting, the ever-resourceful Fr. Ravalli repurposed tin cans as very basic chandeliers. And the blue colored wood is not painted—it is stained with the juice of local berries.

Today Sacred Heart Mission, also known as the Cataldo Mission, is the centerpiece of Idaho's Old Mission State Park. This is no longer an active parish, although religious services are held there from time to time. The mission stands as a testament to the dedication of the Native American Catholics of Idaho, and a tribute to missionaries such as Fr. Ravalli who sacrificed their lives to bring the faith to a far-off country.

ILLINOIS

BELLEVILLE | National Shrine of Our Lady of the Snows
442 S. DeMazenod Dr. • Belleville, IL 62223
618-394-6276 • www.snows.org

When I was a kid in a Catholic school in New Jersey, whenever snow was predicted, my classmates and I would pray to Our Lady of the Snows to turn the predicted flurries into a blizzard so we would have a snow day.
Sometimes, the sister led the prayers (she probably wanted a day off, too).

But Our Lady of the Snows is not the patroness of snow days, she is the patroness of the magnificent Basilica of St. Mary Major in Rome. Furthermore, the Missionary Oblates of Mary Immaculate have a special devotion to her.

According to a very ancient story, on the night of August 4, 352, a well-to-do Roman couple had a vision of the Blessed Mother in which she told them to go the Esquiline Hill the next morning where she would reveal what she wanted. That same night, Mary appeared to Pope Liberius and gave him the same message. The next day, August 5, was a typical sweltering day. Yet when the husband and wife and Pope Liberius and his entourage arrived at the Esquiline, they saw on the hilltop the outline, in snow, of a grand basilica. The couple and the pope put up the money to build on the site a grand basilica in honor of Our Lady.

As for the Oblates and Our Lady of the Snows, devotion to Mary under this title was promoted by an Oblate missionary priest, Fr. Paul Schulte. He was a pilot who flew to Oblate mission sites north of the Arctic Circle, carrying medical supplies and other necessities the missionaries and their congregations needed. Spending so much time in these frozen wastelands brought to Fr. Schulte's mind the story of Our Lady of the Snows.

In 1958, the Oblates, assisted by many laymen and women, planned a shrine to Our Lady of Snows in Belleville, Illinois, on the bluffs above the Mississippi River. There is a main church as well as chapels and a beautifully landscaped outdoor shrine. The Stations of the Cross, for example, display life-size sculptures in individual shrines. The Way of the Cross is a half-mile long, which makes it an easy walk for most pilgrims, but you can also follow the Stations in your car.

A replica of the Lourdes Grotto is another popular outdoor destination for pilgrims. There is an altar in the grotto where Mass can be celebrated (consult the website for Mass times), and recently, brides and grooms have opted to have their wedding ceremony at the grotto.

CHICAGO | Old St. Mary's Church
1500 S. Michigan Ave. • Chicago, IL 60605
312-922-3444 • www.oldstmarys.com

In response to a petition from 128 priestless Chicago Catholics, Bishop Joseph Rosati of St. Louis in 1833 sent them newly ordained Fr. John St. Cyr to start a parish in what was still little more than a frontier outpost—the major American metropolis would come later.

A pressing need was the erection of a suitable chapel where Mass could be said. The first Mass that Father St. Cyr celebrated in Chicago was in the log cabin home of a French settler, Mark Beaubien. Mass in the Beaubien house could only be a temporary fix, so Father St. Cyr went looking for a piece of real estate where he could establish a parish. At the cost of only four hundred dollars, he built his little church—it measured twenty-five by thirty-five feet—at the intersection of Lake and State streets, and he dedicated it to Our Lady under the name of St. Mary of the Assumption.

From the day of Father St. Cyr's inaugural Mass until today, parishioners have worshipped in six different church buildings in six different locations. If you visit the current Church of Old St. Mary's, you won't find much that is truly old. The current church was built in a dramatic, contemporary style; its most prominent features are the sweeping upward lines that direct worshippers' attention up to God, and the large, colorful stained-glass windows that fill the church with color and light.

The style of Old St. Mary's won't be to everyone's taste. Nonetheless, the church has won acclaim from the professionals: for their striking design, Serena and Sturm Architects won the Silver Award from the Association of Licensed Architects.

There are two survivors from earlier incarnations of Old St. Mary's: the altar crucifix and a statue of Our Lady of the Assumption. All of the other artwork is contemporary and was specially commissioned for the current church.

Consult the parish website for Mass times and when the church is open.

CHICAGO | National Shrine of St. Jude / Our Lady of
Guadalupe Church
3200 E. 91st St. • Chicago, IL
312-544-8230 • www.shrineofstjude.org

St. Jude as the patron saint of lost causes is an American phenom-enon (in Europe, desperate Catholics pray to St. Rita). How St. Jude came to be associated with impossible cases is itself impos-sible to pin down, but we do know how devotion to St. Jude first began to spread in the United States.

In the 1920s, the Claretian Fathers staffed Our Lady of Guadalupe Parish on the South Side of Chicago. The neighbor-hood was surrounded by steel mills where many of the parishio-ners worked. During the Depression, the mills started laying off workers. Jobs were scarce, unemployment insurance did not exist yet. Fr. James Tort, the pastor of Our Lady of Guadalupe, began to see many of his parishioners standing on breadlines.

Fr. Tort had a deep devotion to St. Jude, one of Christ's twelve apostles who, as the shrine's website points out, at the time was not widely revered in the Catholic world. At first, he prayed to his favorite saint in private, but as conditions for his unemployed parishioners worsened, Fr. Tort announced a public novena to St. Jude. So many parishioners attended the first novena that Fr. Tort repeated it again and again. The St. Jude novena became a regular part of parish life at Our Lady of Guadalupe.

As stories of answered prayers spread to other Chicago churches, and then across the country, other parishes began novenas to St. Jude. All during the Depression and World War II, and every day since, the priests and people of Our Lady of Guadalupe have gathered in their parish church to ask St. Jude to help them in every temporal and spiritual necessity. Today, Our Lady of Guadalupe is recognized as the National Shrine of St. Jude, and the mail continually brings stories from grateful people who testify that St. Jude helped them at the moment when they had despaired of finding any help.

The church is very simple, inside and out. After the Second Vatican Council, the high altar and most of the communion rail were removed, and a rather plain altar and other furnishings were installed. This may not appeal to pilgrims with a more traditional bent when it comes to church decor. But the shrine of St. Jude still preserves the traditional look, and there is a room filled with row upon row of vigil lights. As you pray before the statue of St. Jude, look below the altar—inside are thousands of prayer requests that come every week from desperate souls. The Claretian Fathers and the parishioners remember these requests in all their Masses and prayers to St. Jude.

CHICAGO | St. John Cantius Church
825 N. Carpenter St. • Chicago, IL 60642
312-243-7373 • www.cantius.org

St. John Cantius is one of the Polish cathedrals that dominate the skyline and once were centers of the spiritual and cultural life of the huge Polish neighborhoods on Chicago's west side. The construction in the 1950s of I-90/Kennedy Expressway blasted through the old Polish area, driving many Polish immigrants and their Polish American children and grandchildren to the suburbs. This exodus sapped the vitality of everything from Polish banks, delis, and restaurants to Polish Catholic parishes; St. John Cantius Parish was one of the victims.

Cantius appeared to be a dying parish. It seemed to the handful of parishioners who still remained that the new pastor, Fr. Frank Phillips, had been sent by the Archdiocese of Chicago to shut the church down. Instead, Fr. Phillips launched an ambitious campaign to revive his parish. He collected funds to make major repairs, such as a new heating system; restore the baroque-style church's works of art; and add more art, including a splendid replica of Veit Stoss's elaborate altarpiece (the original is preserved in the Basilica of St. Mary in Kraków, Poland).

The parish's small museum of sacred art is open on Sundays before Mass and displays other treasures, including a large monstrance fashioned from gold, silver, and precious stones donated by parishioners. Even the church floor is one of Fr. Phillips's projects — he replaced the old vinyl flooring with a fine wooden floor inlaid with emblems of Jesus Christ and the Blessed Virgin Mary.

Cantius's devotion to beauty extends beyond fine works of art to the liturgy and traditional Catholic devotions. Every day, the priests of the parish offer the Novus Ordo, or Ordinary, form of the Mass in English, and the Tridentine, or Extraordinary, form of the Mass in Latin. One of the glories of the parish is its music program, with skilled organists and well-trained parish choirs singing Gregorian chant and masterworks by composers that range from Palestrina to Mozart to the work of modern composers. If you can, make an effort to attend a Sunday Mass — it is an unforgettable experience that will make you envious of Cantius parishioners who have access to such beauty every day.

Typically, Cantius is open all day, but contact the church office to confirm the hours of Masses and other services, as well as when the church is open to visitors.

CHICAGO | Shrine of Christ the King Sovereign Priest
6401 South Woodlawn • Chicago, IL 60637
773-363-7409 • www.institute-christ-king.org/chicago

This is an unusual destination because the church is in ruins and visitors are not permitted inside.

The Shrine of Christ the King Sovereign Priest stands a few blocks south of the University of Chicago. In the first years of its life, it was known as the Church of St. Clara and was staffed by the Carmelites. When the Carmelites left, the church was renamed for St. Gelasius, a pope who died in 496 after reigning for only four years. This is consistent with Chicago's history of naming churches after little-known saints.

As is the case with so many Catholic churches of Chicago's South Side, after years as a thriving parish, the neighborhood and the Church of St. Gelasius went into decline. The fatal blow came in the 1970s when a disastrous fire gutted the interior of the church. The shell of St. Gelasius stood for about three decades until the Archdiocese of Chicago decided that the ruined church would have to be demolished.

Then, according to the shrine's website, in 2004, before the wrecking crew could arrive, priests from the Institute of Christ the King petitioned Cardinal Francis George to let them have the building, which they would restore and open as a shrine parish.

Cardinal George, who had always admired the impressive architecture of St. Gelasius, was pleased to let the Christ the King Fathers try to rebuild the church and revive the parish.

The priests of the Institute celebrate exclusively the old Latin Mass, also known these days as the Extraordinary form of the Mass. Chicago Catholics who loved the old Mass began coming to St. Gelasius on Sundays, and some of them even made the effort to attend Mass on weekdays. The parish began to grow thanks to its commitment to traditional worship, and its outreach to the neighborhood in terms of everything from organizing block cleanup days to hosting civic and neighborhood meetings. The restoration was nearly complete when Cardinal George enthroned above the high altar an eighteenth-century wooden sculpture of the Infant of Prague.

Then tragedy struck again. In October 2015, fire swept through the shrine church, destroying the choir loft and much of the church furnishings, and bringing down the roof.

Defying the danger, firefighters saved the tabernacle, which contained the Blessed Sacrament, and the statue of the Infant of Prague. The statue was damaged in the fire, and so it was sent for restoration to artisans in Germany. It was expected to come home sometime in 2016, but had not yet returned by 2017.

Rather than tear down the church, the archdiocese in 2016 gave the institute of Christ the King the deed to the property. The Christ the King Fathers have found wide support from parishioners, neighbors—including the faculty, staff, and students of the University of Chicago, Chicago area media, as well as supporters who live far from the shrine.

Stop by the church to admire the handsome exterior and perhaps learn how the reconstruction is progressing. Contact the parish office to learn about times and locations of daily Mass. And if you can spare it, make a gift to the church's restoration fund.

St. John | **The Shrine of Christ's Passion**
10630 Wicker Ave. (Rte. 41) • St. John, IN 46373
219-365-6010 • www.shrineofchristspassion.org

This remarkable shrine enables you to walk in the footsteps of Jesus Christ during his final hours—from the Last Supper to his burial. The shrine's moving prayer trail concludes with Our Lord's glorious resurrection.

The life-size sculptures are the work of sculptor Mickey Wells of Texas. They are wonderfully expressive, with details that draw you in to each scene. There is Pontius Pilate just as he lifts his hand from the basin of water and declares that he is innocent of "this just man's blood." As a Roman soldier strips Jesus of his garments, he reveals the wounds from the scourging Christ endured, while on the Lord's face is an expression of sorrow, pain, and humiliation. Perhaps most dramatic of all is Christ being nailed to the cross: A Roman soldier holds down Jesus's arm with his right hand while raising the hammer high above his head with his left. It is a moment frozen in time, just before Christ feels another agonizing blow that will affix him to the cross.

At each station there is a meditation recorded by popular Chicago broadcaster Bill Kurtis that will help you focus on the scene and enrich your visit to the shrine.

On the grounds there is also a Sanctity of Life Shrine, in memory of the innocent victims of abortion.

The shrine is open daily, 10 AM to 5 PM. From June 1 through September 30, the shrine is open in Thursday until 8 PM. On Christmas Eve, the shrine closes at noon. The shrine is closed on New Year's Eve, New Year's Day, Thanksgiving, and Christmas Day.

SAINT MARY-OF-THE-WOODS | Sisters of Providence of Saint Mary-of-the-Woods Motherhouse

1 Sisters of Providence Rd. • Saint Mary-of-the-Woods, IN 47876
812-535-3131 • www.spsmw.org

The motherhouse is the home of the Sisters of Providence, teaching sisters whose order originated in France in the early 1800s. St. Mother Theodore Guerin (Theodore was the name she took when she entered the religious life) came to America in 1840 with five sisters of her order at the request of the bishop of Vincennes, Indiana. Their "convent" and their "chapel" were log cabins in the wilderness. In time, outside Vincennes, at a place they called Saint Mary-of-the-Woods, the sisters built a real convent, a magnificent church, and a school for girls.

The Shrine of St. Mother Theodore Guerin begins with a museum that tells the story of her life in France, her voyage across the Atlantic, and her adventures as a missionary sister in Indiana. At the end of the museum is the chapel where Mother Guerin's remains lie enshrined in a simple-yet-handsome wooden casket.

The motherhouse's chapel is a grand Renaissance-style church dedicated to the Immaculate Conception. The interior is still lovely with its marble carvings, statues, and paintings, but some pilgrims may not care for the stripped-down sanctuary and the sculpture of the risen Christ over the altar that to some eyes will appear to be borderline creepy.

Much more satisfying for pilgrims with a love of traditional church design is the Blessed Sacrament Chapel, where four angels, carved from pure white marble, support the monstrance that displays the Sacred Host. Over this altar is a graceful baldachino, or canopy, supported by beautiful colored marble columns.

After you've prayed in the church and adored the Blessed Sacrament in its chapel, wander around the landscaped grounds to read the markers that trace the history of the sisters at this site, and visit the many shrines erected by the order's benefactors over the decades on the grounds of the motherhouse.

For hours of operation and to learn when Mass is celebrated, contact the motherhouse office.

VINCENNES | Basilica of St. Francis Xavier (the Old Cathedral)
205 Church Street • Vincennes, IN 47591
812-882-5638

Parish churches close all the time—it has been that way almost from the beginning. Populations shift, so parishes move to locations where they can expand. But reducing the liturgical life of a cathedral basilica is rare. Yet that has been the fate of Vincennes' old cathedral, the Basilica of St. Francis Xavier.

Rome made Vincennes a diocese in 1834, and St. Francis Xavier Church, then only eight years old, was chosen as the cathedral of the new diocese. The exterior is very plain—unadorned red brick walls with a white steeple over the main entrance. In niches above the doors are three sculptures: St. Joan of Arc, St. Francis Xavier, and St. Patrick. The statue of St. Joan is a tribute to the French settlers, soldiers, and trappers who were the first parishioners of St. Francis Xavier. It is also the first statue of St. Joan erected in the United States after her canonization in 1920.

Step inside the cathedral, and you'll find yourself inside an early nineteenth-century Catholic jewel box. The ceiling, the statues, the Stations of the Cross, even the organ's pipes are all painted. The original altars and the old bishop's throne have been preserved. A painting of the crucifixion hangs over the high altar, with one of St. Francis Xavier over St. Joseph's altar, and over Our Lady's altar is a third painting showing the patron saints of the first four bishops of Vincennes: Pope St. Celestine, St. Stephen, St. Simon the Apostle, and St. Maurice of the Theban Legion.

The first four bishops are buried in the basilica's undercroft. Enshrined in the undercroft's altar, behind a glass plate, you can see the relics of St. Aufidius, a Roman boy martyred when he was only twelve years old.

Mass is offered at the old cathedral several times a week—contact the office for days, times, and hours when the old cathedral is open to visitors. On the grounds is the old cathedral library, a collection of eleven thousand books and manuscripts. If you are interested in visiting or using the library for research, contact the church office.

IOWA

Peosta | New Melleray Abbey and Retreat House
6632 Melleray Circle • Peosta, IA 52068
563-588-2319 • www.newmelleray.org

New Melleray is a monastery of Trappist monks set amid the rolling farmland south of Dubuque, Iowa. It was founded in 1849 by monks from Mount Melleray Abbey who came from Ireland to Iowa to establish a community  of Trappists in the New World. The rural setting is lovely, and it ensures the peace and silence of life in the abbey—two qualities which all monastic communities of men and women prize.

The church is the heart of the abbey. It is constructed of golden limestone, with heavy wooden beams supporting the vaulted ceiling. It was built in the late nineteenth century in the Gothic style, which at the time was experiencing a revival in Europe and America. An iron grill separates the pews for visitors from the choir where the monks gather eight times a day for Mass and to pray the Divine Office. Guests are invited to join the monks in their daily cycle of prayer, but it is not obligatory. And since the first liturgical office of the day is chanted at 3:30 in the morning (a bell rings at 3:15 AM to rouse the community), retreatants may find it easier to pick and choose when to attend services in the church.

Rooms in the abbey guesthouse are basic—a bed, a desk, a chair—but each room also has a private bathroom. There is a dining room where guests take their meals. Visitors expecting a diet of bread and water and bowls of thin gruel will be pleasantly surprised by the fresh, hearty dishes the monks prepare for their guests.

The guesthouse also has a small library, a guest chapel, meeting rooms, and a coffee room. There are breaks throughout the day when guests can find a quiet place to read, meditate, or pray. And the walks through the countryside are beautiful.

Most guests come to New Melleray for private, unstructured retreats, but themed retreats led by one of the monks are offered from time to time throughout the year. Consult the abbey's website for the dates of upcoming retreats.

To cover their expenses, the monks ask that each guest make a donation of $70 per day. New Melleray is a popular destination for retreats, so it is essential to make a reservation well in advance and to be flexible about dates when you would like to stay at the abbey.

SPILLVILLE | St. Wenceslaus Church
207 Church St. • Spillville, IA 52168
563-562-3637 • www.spillville.org/Church.html

Throughout its history, America has attracted immigrants seeking freedom, safety from persecution, and opportunities that did not exist in their native countries.

In the 1850s, a group of Catholics who had settled in and around Spillville, Iowa, began to erect the first parish in the United States to serve immigrants from Bohemia, now known as the Czech Republic.

Over the next sixteen years the parishioners expanded their church, erecting a bell tower, embellishing the sanctuary, and adding transepts. In 1876, they added an especially significant feature—a church organ. Most Catholic churches have organs, but the organ of St. Wenceslaus is special.

In 1892, the celebrated Czech Catholic composer Antonín Dvořák arrived in New York City with his wife and six children. American music lovers greeted him as a celebrity. Dvořák gave his first public concert at Carnegie Hall, where he conducted his piece, the *Columbian Te Deum*, written in praise of the United States and to celebrate the 400th anniversary of Christopher Columbus's discovery of America.

While living in New York, Dvořák accepted the directorship of the National Conservatory of Music of America, and began composing a series of works based on music unique to America, including African American spirituals, which he called "the Negro melodies." The most famous composition of Dvořák's American period was the *New World Symphony*.

In spring 1893, Dvořák and his wife decided to spend the summer months in Spillville, where they and their children would live in the midst of a now-considerable Czech immigrant community. During his summer vacation in Spilllville, Dvořák continued to compose American-inspired music, including his *American String Quartet*. But Dvořák also found a daily diversion.

As a boy, Dvořák had been trained as an organist, so every morning, he left the house he was renting in Spillville and walked to St. Wenceslaus Church. He climbed up to the choir loft, and as the priest said daily Mass, Dvořák played Czech hymns. The parish still uses the organ that Dvořák played; it was restored and rededicated in 1996.

KANSAS

**PILSEN | St. John Nepomucene Church /
Fr. Emil Kapaun Shrine**
Corner of Remington Road and 275th Street
Pilsen, KS 66861 • 620-382-3369
www.hfpmc.org/churches/st-john-nepomucene-pilsen
www.fatherkapaun.org

Pilsen is small rural town, once the home of a large number of immigrants from Bohemia, now part of the Czech Republic. The steeple of St. John Nepomucene Church dominates the local skyline today as it has since the church was first erected in 1915.

Inside, the original altars—elaborately carved in the Gothic style—the brightly colored statues and Stations of the Cross, and the luminous stained glass windows are all in excellent condition. The church is almost exactly as it appeared during the short period of time when one of St. John's parishioners, Fr. Emil Kapaun, was pastor here.

After the outbreak of the Korean War, Fr. Kapaun volunteered to serve as an army chaplain. In 1950, after only a few months of service on the front lines, he and about one thousand American soldiers were captured by North Korean troops and taken to a prison camp. Conditions at the camp were terrible: the POW huts were unheated, there were no medical facilities (the camp "hospital" was a place where the dying were abandoned by the guards to die), and there was not enough food.

Fr. Kapaun led his fellow POWs in prayer, consoled them, and nursed the sick as best he could. After dark, he would sneak out of his hut and raid the guard's supply shed for rations. Before each of his raids, Fr. Kapaun prayed to St. Dismas, the good thief.

In May 1951, Fr. Kapaun was so ill the North Korean guards forced him to move to the "hospital," where he died.

The men he served with never forgot him, and for decades, they petitioned the Church in the United States to advance Fr. Kapaun's cause for sainthood. In 1993, Rome recognized his apparent holiness by granting him the title "Servant of God" and opening an examination of his life and virtues. In 2013, Fr. Kapaun was awarded the Medal of Honor.

There are tributes to Fr. Kapaun inside the church. In the rectory is a small museum that displays items that belonged to him. To visit the church and the museum, contact the parish office in advance for a guided tour.

KENTUCKY

BARDSTOWN | Basilica of St. Joseph Proto-Cathedral
310 West Stephen Foster Ave. • Bardstown, KY 40004
502-348-3126 • http://www.stjosephbasilica.org/

It must have come as a surprise to the Catholic settlers of Kentucky when the pope made Bardstown a diocese, with Fr. Benedict Joseph Flaget, an émigré from France, appointed bishop. It was a daunting assignment—Bishop Flaget was responsible for a diocese that extended from Detroit down to New Orleans, and from the Allegheny Mountains westward across the Mississippi River to Missouri.

It was Bishop Flaget who decided to build, as the spiritual heart of his diocese, the handsome red-brick, Greek-Revival cathedral of St. Joseph that you can see today.

To build such a church was an expensive proposition, and since most of the congregants were cash poor, instead of dollars they contributed their labor, baking bricks on the grounds and cutting down trees for lumber, including the columns that support the arches inside the church. Clever pioneers that they were, they covered the columns with plaster, then painted them to pass for marble. The bottom of one of the columns has been exposed, which reveals the original poplar log that was harvested for the church sometime between 1816 and 1819.

Early in its history, Pope Leo XII, King Louis-Philippe of France, and King Francis I of the Kingdom of the Two Sicilies donated paintings to adorn the cathedral, including a painting of the coronation of the Blessed Virgin by Murillo, and three paintings by van Dyck. Queen Maria Amalia and the ladies of the French court embroidered vestments, and the royal couple also donated sacred vessels for the celebration of Mass. This collection of paintings from the 1600s is one the treasures of the Catholic Church in America, so make room in your travel schedule for a tour of this remarkable cathedral.

Contact the parish office for Mass times, when the cathedral is open to visitors, and how to arrange a tour of the church.

LOUISVILLE | St. Martin of Tours Church
639 South Shelby St. • Louisville, KY 40202
502-582-2827 • www.stmartinoftourschurch.org

Aside from the handsome stone front, the exterior of the sides and back of St. Martin of Tours Church are so austere—and could even be described as "bare"— that you could be forgiven for cruising right by the place. But that would be a mistake, because inside is one of those glorious churches from the 1800s that are not made anymore. Everywhere there are colorful statues of saints, glowing stained glass windows, and altars carved in the Gothic style.

One of the chief treasures of the church, treasures that set St. Martin's apart from most Catholic churches in America, are the skeletons of two martyrs from the years of the Roman persecution of the Church—St. Magnus, a Roman soldier, and St. Bonosa, a Roman woman who consecrated her virginity to Christ. The relics arrived in the parish in 1902, the gift of Pope Leo XIII. They are enshrined behind plate glass beneath the church's side altars.

St. Martin's is famous in Louisville and the surrounding area for its magnificent organ, which arrived from Germany sometime after 1861. The church also is renowned for its solemn Sunday Masses—one Novus Ordo, or the Ordinary form, the second the Traditional Latin Mass, or Extraordinary form. It is worth making an effort to attend either of these Masses.

When we think of places in America with large Catholic populations, Kentucky is probably not high on our list. Yet in St. Martin's, we see the effort and generosity of our Catholic ancestors who built in Louisville a worthy house for God.

NEW HAVEN | Abbey of Our Lady of Gethsemani
3642 Monks Rd. • New Haven, KY 40051
General Information: 502-549-3117
Retreat Reservations: 502-549-4133 • www.monks.org

It's impossible to hear the name "Abbey of Gethsemani" and not think of Thomas Merton, a Trappist monk of the abbey, a writer, social activist, mystic, and one of the greatest influences on twentieth- and twenty-first century American Catholicism.

Merton first visited the abbey in 1941 and, later that year, joined the community of Trappist monks at Gethsemani. As a monk, he took the name "Louis," and, in time, he was ordained to the priesthood.

The abbot of Gethsemani put to good use Fr. Louis's gift as a writer. Initially, he had him translate spiritual and mystical works;

then the abbot urged Merton to write his autobiography. The result was *The Seven Storey Mountain*, a bestseller that has become a spiritual classic for Catholics and non-Catholics alike. Since its publication in 1948, it has sold over a million copies.

Over the next twenty years, Fr. Louis wrote about the contemplative life, but he also tackled the controversial issues of his day, from civil rights to resistance to the Vietnam War to the threat of nuclear war.

Trappists have been at Gethsemani for more than 150 years, and the abbey, as it appears today, is very simple, in keeping with the Trappist tradition of austerity so there are minimal distractions as they strive to maintain a constant conversation with God.

There is the opportunity to walk the grounds within the abbey's walls. And just beyond those walls are paths suitable for prayerful reflection. The hermitage, a small wooden building behind the abbey walls where Merton used to write, is still there.

The monks welcome visitors, whether you are coming for a brief visit, a day to renew your spiritual life, or a longer retreat during the week or over the weekend. Retreatants stay in simply furnished rooms, all of which have their own bathroom. Guests are welcome to participate in the liturgical life of the monks, including daily Mass and the daily recitation of the Divine Office. Confession and consultation with one of the monks are also available.

Gethsemani is a wonderful place to rediscover the voice of God in the silence of the abbey, and to become re-acquainted with Thomas Merton, one of the twentieth century's greatest champions of the monastic life.

LOUISIANA

New Orleans | Cathedral-Basilica of St. Louis King of France
615 Pere Antoine Alley • New Orleans, LA 70116
504-525-9585 • www.stlouiscathedral.org

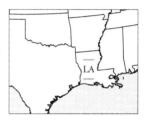

This cathedral is a New Orleans icon. Location has a lot to do with that—St. Louis stands on the edge of Jackson Square (named for a sculpture of General Andrew Jackson perched on a rearing horse). The square is the heart of the Vieux Carre, or Old Quarter, more commonly known as the French Quarter.

Flanking the cathedral are two twin buildings—the Cabildo, built as the seat of city government, and the Presbytere, which was intended as a residence for the cathedral clergy but became an indoor market instead. Along the sides of the square are some of the classic New Orleans townhouses with lacy wrought-iron balconies. Across the square from the cathedral is the levee that overlooks the Mississippi River. And then there is a Jackson Square landmark that almost rivals the fame of St. Louis: Café du Monde, renowned for its chicory coffee and its beignets. The cafe is open twenty-four hours a day, and only closes on Christmas Day and during hurricanes.

The church you see today was designed by Benjamin Latrobe, one of the most distinguished architects in America, who had a hand in designing the US Capitol, the White House, and the

Cathedral of St. Mary of the Assumption in Baltimore, among other American landmarks.

The painted sculptures above the high altar represent the three theological virtues: faith, hope, and charity. Flanking the altar are sculptures of St. Peter and St. Paul.

It's hard to look away from the elegant exterior of the cathedral, but tear yourself away and go inside. You can purchase a brochure for a self-guided tour or ask one of the docents to show you around. The ceiling and upper walls are decorated with paintings of saints. Over the high altar is a mural of the church's patron, St. Louis, king of France. But best of all are the murals of angels and the patron saints of music painted on an arch above the cathedral's organ.

New Orleans | Shrine of Our Lady of Prompt Succor
2701 State St. • New Orleans, LA 70118
504-866-1472 • www.shrineofourladyofpromptsuccor.com

On January 7, 1815, on the outskirts of New Orleans, General Andrew Jackson assembled his motley army of militiamen, civilians, African American slaves, and pirates (under the pirate captain Jean Laffite). Jackson's 3,500 men dug in and prepared to face an army of 13,000 British.

Back in the city, the Ursuline nuns and many citizens of New Orleans crowded into the sisters' chapel to pray before the statue of Our Lady of Prompt Succor (which means "quick help"). The Ursulines made a vow to the Blessed Mother: if, by her prayers, she secured victory for the Americans, the nuns would have a Mass offered every year on the anniversary of the battle.

Religious and laity prayed throughout the night. The shrine's website tells how at dawn, as a priest said Mass, a messenger ran into the chapel with the news that Jackson had defeated the British in a fight that lasted twenty-five minutes.

Ironically, the war was already over—representatives of the American and British governments had signed a peace treaty in Ghent, Belgium, on Christmas Eve, just fifteen days earlier. Given the limitations of travel in 1815, there was no way that news of the peace could have gotten from Ghent to New Orleans in time to stop the battle.

The sisters kept their promise. To this day, a Mass of Thanksgiving commemorating the Battle of New Orleans is still celebrated at the National Shrine of Our Lady of Prompt Succor on the grounds of the Ursuline Academy.

The sculpture of Our Lady holding the Christ Child in her arms is enthroned above the high altar. Mary's robes have been gilded, and she and Jesus both wear elaborate crowns. The chapel's stained glass windows depict scenes from the life of the Blessed Virgin. Especially touching is the window of St. John the Evangelist giving Holy Communion to Our Lady.

The shrine has a busy schedule of Masses, adoration of the Blessed Sacrament, recitation of the rosary, and the Perpetual Novena to Our Lady of Prompt Succor.

The shrine is open weekdays 10 AM until after the 5 PM Mass; Saturday 10:30 AM until after the 11:30 AM Mass; Sunday 8:30 AM until after the 9:30 AM Mass. Contact the shrine office to confirm hours of operation, and to schedule a tour of the shrine.

NEW ORLEANS | Tomb of Venerable Henriette Delille, St.
Louis Cemetery No. 2, Nuns Section
720 St. Louis St. • New Orleans, LA 70119
504-482-5065
www.nolacatholiccemeteries.org/cemeteries/st-louis-cemetery-2

For centuries, visitors to New Orleans have observed that the city is not like other cities in America. Its culture, music, architecture, cuisine, racial and ethnic background of the natives, and deeply rooted Catholicism of the place (look at the flag of Louisiana—the image of the pelican nursing her young with its own blood is an ancient symbol of the Eucharist) all come together to create one of the most fascinating cities in America.

Even the New Orleans cemeteries are unusual. Given the city's very high water table, in-ground burial is out of the question, so the dead are entombed in above-ground mausoleums. You'll find Mother Henriette's tomb in the Nuns Section of St. Louis Cemetery No. 2.

There is a complication with this form of burial, especially if the person in the tomb is a candidate for sainthood. For the sake of space, it has been the custom in New Orleans to bury many people in the same tomb. As a result, Mother Henriette shares her tomb with several other nuns. Identifying the remains of the candidate for sainthood is part of the canonization process, so the tomb has been opened and several skulls retrieved, with the hope that by comparing the DNA of the skulls with the DNA of descendants of the Delille family, the sisters will have a major relic of their founder.

Venerable Henriette Delille (1812–1863) was a child of New Orleans society. Her great-great grandmother was an African who was kidnapped, carried across the Atlantic, and sold into slavery. By the time Henriette was born, her family had bought their freedom and moved in both black and white social circles. Henriette could claim to have African, French, and Spanish blood.

Her mother, a refined, educated, beautiful woman, had been the concubine, or common-law wife, of a Creole. Madame Delille had Henriette trained in music, dancing, French literature—in other words, all the refinements that would enable her to find a wealthy white man who would take her as his common-law wife and give her a financially secure life.

Although she attended the lessons, Henriette rejected the life her mother had planned for her. Instead, with a handful of friends, all of them free people of color, she adopted a way of life that was the polar opposite of her mother's. She devoted herself to nursing the sick, teaching the Catholic faith to free and enslaved children and adults of color, and she and her companions opened the first Catholic home for the elderly in the United States.

Mother Henriette's religious order, the Sisters of the Holy Family, is rather small—about two hundred members today. But like Venerable Henriette herself, they are a vital part of the story of New Orleans.

Open Monday through Saturday 9 AM to 3 PM, Sunday 9 AM to 1 PM.

Sᴛ. Bᴇɴᴇᴅɪᴄᴛ | St. Joseph Abbey
75376 River Rd. • St. Benedict, LA 70457
985-867-2299 • www.saintjosephabbey.com

S t. Joseph Abbey, located near the town of Covington, is a
masterpiece not to be missed. Inside the church and the refectory, or monks' dining room, are dozens of murals, the work of
Dom Gregory de Wit, a Dutch Benedictine monk who spent ten
years living and painting in the abbey. Visitors comment on the
vivid colors of the murals, and there is good reason for that—rather
than rely on store-bought paints which tend to fade or grow dull
over time, Dom Gregory mixed his own pigments, achieving a
level of brilliancy that is exceptional.

During your visit, you are likely to see young men doing maintenance work inside and outside the abbey. These are aspiring
priests who are being educated and trained in the Seminary
College attached to the abbey. The seminarians are like other
college students: they attend classes, but they also participate in
athletics and other extracurricular activities. What sets them apart
is that they are being trained by the faculty to deepen their relationship with God and prepare for life as Benedictine monks.

The motto St. Benedict, the founder of the Benedictines, gave
to his brothers is *ora et labora* ("pray and work"). More than 1,500
years later, the monks and seminarians follow this maxim. From
dawn until sunset, they gather again and again in the church
to recite or chant the Divine Office. They also study theology
and philosophy—not just the seminarians, but also the monks
who have taken their vows, because the education of a monk is

a life-long vocation. In addition, the seminarians and the monks perform all the tasks that keep this big "house" running.

Before you go, stroll over to the abbey cemetery, where you'll find the grave of the National Book Award–winning author Walker Percy. In its May 11, 1990, obituary for Percy, *The New York Times* described him as "a Southern author who wrote about modern man's search for faith and love in a chaotic world." Readers and critics knew Percy for his best-selling, highly acclaimed novels, such as *The Moviegoer*. Few in the literary world knew that Percy had become an Oblate of the Benedictine order, affiliated with St. Joseph's Abbey. As an Oblate, Percy promised to try to live as closely as possible the Rule of St. Benedict.

Retreatants have always been welcome at St. Joseph—it is part of the tradition established by St. Benedict to welcome each guest as if he or she were Christ. Early in 2016, the abbey suffered serious damage from a devastating flood. Before you show up at the monks' doorstep, contact the abbey to check if the guesthouse is ready for visitors.

MAINE

Madison | **Fr. Sebastian Rasle Monument**
St. Sebastian Cemetery • Father Rasle Road
Madison, ME 04950
www.madisonmaine.com/index.php/play/
history/110-old-point-monument

Spelling is an issue at this historic site. Fr. Sebastian's surname is sometimes spelled Rasle and other times Rale or Rasles. The Native American tribe to whom he brought the Catholic faith are known as Abenaki, which is a member of the Wabanaki Confederacy of tribes.

Fr. Rasle was a Jesuit priest who left his home in France to serve as a missionary in New France. The French had definite ideas about what constituted New France—to their mind, it covered all of Canada, and ran down to New Orleans. It also included what is now the state of Maine. English settlers in Massachusetts disputed the French claim, insisting that Maine belonged to the British Crown. When word reached the English in Boston that a French Jesuit had established a mission among the Abenaki in the village of Norridgewock (now within the boundaries of the town of Madison), they launched several expeditions to drive out the Native Americans and capture Fr. Rasle.

Three times over a period of two decades, Fr. Rasle and his congregation were warned that the English were coming and escaped into the woods. The English looted and burned the village, so the Abenaki retaliated by attacking English settlements in southern Maine; the conflict dragged on for years with no hope of a peaceful resolution.

In 1724, the English launched another attack, and this time they took the residents of Norridgewock by surprise. In volley after volley of musket fire, the English killed twenty-five warriors, and wounded another fourteen. They also killed Fr. Rasle.

Later, members of the tribe said that Fr. Rasle had died at the foot of the large wooden cross he had erected in the center of the village. In the English version of the priest's death, he had holed up in his residence, firing upon the attackers. As the English burst through the door, they found Fr. Rasle reloading his musket. They shot him dead where he stood.

All of the dead, including Fr. Rasle were scalped by the English, and the scalps were delivered to government officials in Boston.

A couple days after the attack, those Abenaki who had managed to escape into the forest returned to bury their dead. They laid the body of Fr. Rasle under the altar in his burned-out chapel.

No one knows the place of Fr. Rasle's grave, but there is an obelisk on the site of Norridgewock that Bishop Benedict Fenwick of Boston dedicated in 1833. Two other monuments stand nearby, one that commemorates the school Fr. Rasle founded for the Abenaki, and another raised in his memory by the Daughters of the American Revolution.

The story of the Abenaki and Fr. Rasle and the English gives us insight into how complex, not to mention dangerous, life could be in New England in the late 1600s and early 1700s. The English saw the Native Americans and their Jesuit priest as a threat. The Abenaki viewed the English attacks as unprovoked invasions of their homeland. Whether Fr. Rasle countenanced the retaliatory raids on English is an open question and unlikely to be resolved—just like the conflicting stories of how he died.

What is clear, however, is that Fr. Rasle was one of a continual stream of Jesuits who left comfortable lives in France to plant the faith in the American wilderness.

NEWCASTLE | St. Patrick Church
380 Academy Hill Rd. • Newcastle, ME 04553
207-563-3240 • www.allsaintsmaine.com/st-patrick-history

A quiet country road near the coast of Maine is an unlikely place to find the oldest Catholic church in New England.

St. Patrick Church was built in this out-of-the-way location to serve Irish immigrants, most of whom had come up from Boston to work in the mills founded by two Irishmen, James Kavanagh and Matthew Cottrill. Kavanagh and Cottrill did well in Newcastle, and each donated $1,000 for the construction and furnishing of a church (the contractor estimated the finished church would cost $3,000, so the donations from Kavanagh and Cottrill were substantial).

The red brick church was built in the simple yet elegant Federal style, which, after the American Revolution, was considered suitable for a republic that wanted to differentiate itself from the fancier flourishes of Europe—and that included European architecture.

The inside is simple, too, although with many wonderful little touches. The high altar is in the shape of a Roman sarcophagus. There are only two other sarcophagus altars in America—one in the crypt of Boston's Holy Cross Cathedral, the other in the Mission Church of Santa Barbara in Santa Barbara, California.

Over the altar is a painting of Christ's body being taken down from the cross. It was the gift of the mother of Fr. Jean Louis Cheverus, a French immigrant who became St. Patrick's first pastor. The work reveals the religious devotion of the lady, even if the painting itself is a little on the rough, unsophisticated side.

On either side of the altar are doors, above which are head-boards carved with green sprigs and a golden harp—the traditional emblem of Ireland. Look above the windows and you'll see shields painted blue with a gold cross on each—these are the original Stations of the Cross. The engravings you see on the walls were Stations that were the gift of Bishop James Healy.

One of St. Patrick's greatest historical treasures is the bell hanging in the steeple. It was cast by Paul Revere, and is one of his last completed commissions—Revere died soon after the bell arrived at St. Patrick's.

A declining population and fewer priests have compelled the Diocese of Portland to bundle churches into a single parish. Seven churches, including St. Patrick's, have consolidated into All Saints Parish. Mass is still celebrated at St. Patrick's—call to learn the times of Mass when the church is open to visitors.

South Portland | Grave of Bishop James A. Healy
Calvary Cemetery • 1461 Broadway
South Portland, ME 04106 • 207-773-5796
www.portlanddiocese.org/cemeteries-and-funerals/
calvary-cemetery-of-south-portland-maine

James Healy was the eldest of ten children, the son of Michael Healy, an Irish immigrant, and one of Michael's slaves, Mary Eliza. From all accounts, the couple's relationship was a love affair, but at the time, neither the state nor any church would perform an interracial marriage.

And the situation got worse once the children began to arrive. Under the laws of the state of Georgia (the location of the Healy plantation), all of the offspring of Michael and Mary Eliza were considered illegitimate slaves who were barred from learning to read and write. To save their children from a life of slavery, Michael and Mary Eliza sent their children, one by one, north to Massachusetts where slavery had been abolished.

James Healy studied at Holy Cross College in Worcester, then went to France, where he entered the Sulpician Seminary and was ordained a priest. He returned to America and settled in Boston, where he served the Catholics of that diocese for twenty-one years.

Fr. Healy's mother was of mixed race, and the priest himself had such a fair complexion that he passed for white. In fact, he identified himself as white, and that is how his religious superiors, his friends, and even complete strangers viewed him.

In 1875, Blessed Pope Pius IX named Fr. Healy bishop of the diocese of Maine and New Hampshire. As is the case with so many bishops assigned to frontier territory in the nineteenth century, Bishop Healy worked tirelessly to build up the Church in his diocese. Over a period of twenty-five years, he founded sixty churches, eighteen schools, and opened countless convents and charitable institutions.

At his death in 1900, Bishop Healy was buried in the section of Calvary Cemetery reserved for diocesan priests and the Sisters of Mercy. His grave is easy to spot—it is the one marked by a tall Celtic cross.

Open daily from 8 AM to 3 PM. Call the cemetery office to confirm opening hours and to ask for directions to Bishop Healy's grave.

BALTIMORE | Basilica of the National Shrine of the Assumption of the Blessed Virgin Mary
409 Cathedral St. • Baltimore, MD 21201
410-727-3564 • www.americasfirstcathedral.org

In 1789 Rome named Father John Carroll of Maryland America's first Catholic bishop. Of course, as a bishop, Carroll needed a cathedral, and there was no such thing in the United States at this time. He also needed an architect,  and the finest architect in America, Benjamin Latrobe, offered his services for free.

Latrobe's first design was a church built in the Gothic style, but Bishop Carroll was not a fan of Gothic—it struck him as too medieval, too Old World. America had just formed a government inspired by the ancient Roman republic, and Carroll wanted a cathedral that reflected America's principles.

Latrobe's second design fit the bishop's requirements: he suggested a cathedral built in the style of a Roman temple, with a vast dome inspired by the magnificent dome of the Pantheon in Rome. He selected silvery-gray stone for the church's exterior, and a palette of light, cool colors for the interior. Built into the dome were skylights that flooded the cathedral with natural light.

The cathedral—a basilica since 1937—is so rich in history, fine works of art, and, of course, Latrobe's superb architecture, that the best way to appreciate the beauty and significance of this place is to join a tour. Consult the basilica's website for days and times of guided tours.

Don't miss the museum—it is filled with church treasures that date back to the 1600s. And adjacent to the basilica you'll find the Pope John Paul II Prayer Garden, a green oasis in the heart of downtown Baltimore.

Open Monday through Friday, 7 AM to 4 PM; Saturday 7 AM until the conclusion of the 5:30 PM Mass; Sunday 7 AM until the conclusion of the 4:30 PM Mass.

BALTIMORE | Mother Mary Elizabeth Lange Monument
Perkins Spring Square Park
George Street and Myrtle Avenue • Baltimore, MD 21201

CHAPEL OF OUR LADY OF MOUNT PROVIDENCE
701 Gun Rd. • Baltimore, MD 21227
410-242-6861 • www.oblatesisters.com

In 2000 then Mayor Martin O'Malley, on behalf of the people of Baltimore, unveiled a monument dedicated to Mother Mary Elizabeth Lange and the religious order she founded, the Oblate Sisters of Providence.

Mother Lange grew up in Haiti as the child of a free family of color. To escape the revolution in Haiti, she emigrated to America and settled in Baltimore. There, with the encouragement of Fr. James Joubert—also a refugee from Haiti—and with three free women of African descent, Mother Lange founded the first black religious order. Near the monument was St. Frances Academy, the first school for black children in the United States.

Although Mother Lange envisioned her community as an order of teaching sisters, as was so often the case in America in the 1800s, the nuns went where they were needed, nursing the sick poor, taking in black orphans, even running the household of Baltimore's St. Mary's Seminary.

Mother Lange's greatest champion was St. John Neumann, at the time one of the superiors of the Redemptorists and later bishop of Philadelphia. St. John's enthusiasm for the work of the Sisters of Providence was unusual—most American Church leaders paid little or no attention to black Catholics. There may have been a racist undercurrent to this, but the bishops were also preoccupied with increasing the number of priests who would serve the Irish and German immigrants who were coming to America by the tens of thousands.

Mother Lange's community lives on today. In 1991 her cause for canonization was introduced in Rome, and in 2003 her remains were exhumed and enshrined in the Chapel of Our Lady of Mount Providence in the sisters' Baltimore motherhouse.

St. Clement's Island | St. Clement's Island Museum
38370 Point Breeze Rd
Colton's Point, MD 20626
301-769-2222
www.co.saint-marys.md.us/recreate/stclementsisland.asp

It will take a little effort to visit St. Clement's Island. There is no bridge from the mainland; however, the museum runs a water taxi—call in advance for days and times of operation.

St. Clement's is uninhabited, but its significance is not lost on lovers of history, especially Catholic history. On March 25, 1634, the Feast of the Annunciation, about 140 colonists (most of whom were not Catholic) disembarked from their ships, the Ark and the Dove, and came ashore on this island. The Catholic colonists chose to name the place in honor of St. Clement because they had set sail from England on November 23, St. Clement's feast day, and because he is the patron saint of seafarers.

Once ashore, the colonists erected a large log cross and a rough-hewn altar where Fr. Andrew White, SJ, celebrated Mass. Marylanders trace their origins to the arrival of these colonists, and March 25 is still observed as Maryland Day.

The Catholic settlers had come armed with a charter from King Charles I guaranteeing them liberty to practice their religion freely in the colony—something denied them back home in England. The colonists, acting on their own initiative, issued a decree that granted freedom of religion to Christians of any denomination.

Exhibits in the museum chronicle the religious and political tensions in England in the sixteenth and seventeenth centuries, the settlement of Maryland, and the English settlers' negotiations with the Native Americans in the region for land. The museum also displays a twenty-foot-long mural of the early history of colonial Maryland.

The museum is open daily from 10 AM to 5 PM. It is closed from January 4 to March 24, as well as on New Year's Day, Thanksgiving Day, the day after Thanksgiving, Christmas Eve, and Christmas Day.

EMMITSBURG | Basilica of the National Shrine of
St. Elizabeth Ann Seton
339 South Seton Ave. • Emmitsburg, MD 21727
301-447-6606 • www.setonshrine.org

If you are visiting Gettysburg, Pennsylvania, take a morning or afternoon and drive down Route 15—it's a straight shot, about thirty minutes long, through largely open country to the Mother Seton Shrine. If you're coming from Baltimore, it is about sixty miles away.

Mother Seton and fifteen companions came to this spot on the outskirts of Emmitsburg in 1809. They moved into what is known as the Stone House, a building that dated to the 1700s. The building you can see today was expanded—the sisters had no choice, since the original house had only four rooms, two upstairs, two downstairs, and a tiny room that they used as a chapel (how sixteen women squeezed inside this miniscule chapel is a mystery).

Then walk over to the much more spacious White House. The sisters have furnished it exactly as it would have looked in the early 1800s when Mother Seton and her nuns lived, taught classes, and prayed here. The much more spacious chapel has been preserved. Look at the altar rail—a plaque marks the spot where Mother Seton knelt every morning to receive Communion.

Behind the White House is the sisters' cemetery, where you'll see the graves of Mother Seton's sister-in-law, Harriet, and her daughter, Anna Maria. In the cemetery is a red brick Mortuary Chapel built in the Gothic style. Mother Seton's son, William, had this chapel built to enshrine her remains.

The basilica is built in the Byzantine style, and as is the case with all Byzantine churches it has a splendid mosaic over the altar. You'll find Mother Seton's tomb along the side aisle. Behind the panel that bears her name are the relics of Mother Seton resting in a small copper casket.

Go down to the lower level of the basilica and explore the museum that traces the lives of Mother Seton's family—her parents, her husband, her children, her in-laws. Using images, fascinating stories, and countless artifacts that belonged to the Bayley and Seton families, this permanent collection tells the story of Elizabeth Ann Bayley, her girlhood as a member of a well-to-do New York Episcopalian family, her marriage to an up-and-coming young merchant, the birth of her children, her husband's financial troubles (made worse when he contracted tuberculosis), and his early death.

At the beginning of her widowhood, Mother Seton took an interest in the Catholic faith; she was especially drawn to the sacrament of confession and the real presence of Christ in the Eucharist. When she converted to Catholicism, her relatives and friends virtually disowned her. (The animosity most Americans felt toward the Catholic Church made life difficult for converts, such as the widow Seton.)

With the help of Bishop John Carroll, who invited her to come to Baltimore and support herself as a schoolteacher, Seton began to see a new direction for her life. She founded the first order of sisters in America, and the school they opened in Emmitsburg was the beginning of the parochial school system in the United States.

The basilica is open almost every day of the year from 10:00 AM to 4:30 PM. Guided tours are available at 10 AM, 11 AM, 1 PM, 2 PM, 3 PM. Call to confirm Mass times, tour times, and if any special events are schedule at the shrine during your visit.

St. Mary's City | Historic St. Mary's City
18559 Hogaboom Lane • St. Mary's City, MD 20686
240-895-4990 • www.hsmcdigshistory.org

If you liked Colonial Williamsburg in Virginia, or Plimoth Plantation in Massachusetts, chances are that you'll enjoy a visit to Historic St. Mary's City. Like Williamsburg and Plimoth, St. Mary's is a living history museum where reenactors in full seventeenth-century dress go about the business of day-to-day life as the early settlers of Maryland would have done in the 1600s.

During the political upheaval of the late 1600s, the Protestant majority in the colony (whom the Catholic founders of Maryland had welcomed) staged a coup, seized the government, overturned the edict that granted religious liberty at all Christians, and plundered and burned a good part of St. Mary's City. Soon thereafter, the residents abandoned the town and scattered. As a result, the city that you see today is a careful reconstruction based on a thorough study of the site by trained archaeologists.

One site to which you'll be drawn is the Brick or Jesuit Chapel. It was reconstructed on the original foundations, and the artifacts discovered at the site are exhibited next to the chapel in a separate building. There is also fascinating information about the discovery of three lead coffins bearing the remains of Philip and Anne Calvert (the Calverts were a noble English family who served as governors of Maryland) and the remains of an unidentified child.

You can explore this historic site on your own, or for something more in-depth, make a reservation for an adult tour or a youth tour—or treat yourself and your children to both.

St. Mary's City is significant for many reasons: it is the site of the first Catholic chapel in the English colonies, the first colony to recognize freedom of conscience, the first colony to establish the separation of church and state. It was also the home of some remarkable individuals, including Margaret Brent, the first woman to demand the right to vote, and Mathias de Sousa, the first African American to hold public office in British America.

MASSACHUSETTS

Boston | Great Elm Monument, Boston Common
Boston Common • 139 Tremont St.
Boston, MA 02111 • www.boston.gov/parks/boston-common

Boston Common is America's oldest public park, a fifty-acre, oddly shaped, five-sided polygon, bordered by Beacon, Park, Tremont, Boylston, and Arlington streets, in the heart of the historic city.

At or near the center of the Common is a plaque that marks the spot where the Great Elm stood until 1876, a landmark in old Boston that natives used to describe as the city's oldest inhabitant. Among its other uses, the Common was the site of public hangings, and there is a tradition that the Great Elm was used as gallows. One of the most notorious executions said to have taken place at the elm (or near it) was the hanging of Ann Glover in 1688.

Glover was an Irish Catholic who, with her husband, had been rounded up by Oliver Cromwell's troops and shipped off to the Caribbean, where they became indentured servants. It is also possible that they were sold into slavery. At some point, Glover came to Boston, perhaps taken there by John Goodwin, who may have purchased her outright or purchased her indenture. There are a lot of holes in this story.

At the Goodwin home, among her other duties, Glover cared for the five Goodwin children and did the family laundry. One day Martha Goodwin, age thirteen, accused Glover of stealing laundry. The accusation led to a nasty argument between Glover and Martha and ended with the Goodwin children accusing Glover of bewitching them.

Glover was arrested and put on trial. She must have had a defiant streak, because although she spoke and understood English, she would only answer the court's questions in her native Irish. According to Mary Rezac, writing in 2014 in an article entitled "Was the last witch of Boston actually a Catholic martyr?" (*Catholic News Agency*), all of the evidence suggests that Ann's real crime was her Catholicism. At the time, Catholic priests and Catholic churches were outlawed in Massachusetts.

Ann was known to not only refuse to attend the Puritan church, but had been seen saying her rosary, which apparently was enough to make the town's magistrates conclude that she was flouting their authority. According to Boston City Council records, the notorious witch hunter, Cotton Mather, denounced Ann at her trial as "a scandalous old Irishwoman...a Roman Catholic and obstinate in idolatry." Ann Glover was sentenced to death by hanging. She was executed on November 16. In 1988 on the 300th anniversary of her execution, the Boston City Council established November 16 as Goody Glover Day (women in seventeenth-century Massachusetts were often addressed as "Goodwife"—"Goody" was the informal form). It is said that she was buried in an unmarked grave in the Granary Burying Ground across the street from the Common.

BOSTON | Kennedy/Fitzgerald Walking Tour
Tour offered through the National Park Service
www.nps.gov/jofi/planyourvisit/north-end-tour.htm

There was a time when to all the world the family of Joseph P. Kennedy Sr. and his wife, Rose Fitzgerald Kennedy, seemed to be the epitome of what a big, successful, devout Catholic clan ought to be. They had nine (count 'em!) children. Rose had been named a papal countess by Pope Pius XII (who, in a chapel in the Vatican, gave the Kennedy's youngest son, Teddy, his First Holy Communion).

Over time, it was revealed that the big, happy, confident Catholic family was a public-relations gimmick, and the tales of scandals, especially among the Kennedy sons, pulled them off their pedestal as the leaders of America's Catholic aristocracy. Nonetheless, the Kennedys continue to be a source of fascination, and romance—it's not unusual even today for the three years when John F. Kennedy and his First Lady Jacqueline Bouvier Kennedy occupied the White House to be referred to as "Camelot," an allusion not only the to the Arthur and Guinevere legend, but also to the hit Broadway musical of the time, starring Julie Andrews and Richard Burton.

Joseph was an enormous success on Wall Street and in Hollywood; Rose was beautiful, well educated, and had the gracious social polish she had acquired at finishing schools in Europe. Yet because they were Irish and Catholic, the Kennedys and the Fitzgeralds never managed to gain acceptance among the Boston Brahmins, the city's Protestant elite. That is why this walking tour will take you primarily to old immigrant areas such the North End rather than to the mansions of Beacon Hill.

As it happens, most of these sites follow the Freedom Trail, so you can combine your Kennedy/Fitzgerald walking tour with a tour of Boston's most renowned historic sites.

The JFK Statue

Begin at the State House on Beacon Street—the fathers of both Joseph and Rose served here in the legislature. On the grounds, among other sculptures, is a bronze statue of JFK, and although it shows him in midstride, it falls short of capturing the youthful enthusiasm Kennedy brought to the White House.

MASSACHUSETTS STATE HOUSE

24 Beacon St. • Boston, MA 02133

617-722-2000

www.thefreedomtrail.org/freedom-trail/state-house.shtml

The Omni Parker House

This landmark Boston hotel opened its doors in 1855. It has so many associations with the Kennedys and the Fitzgeralds that it is near impossible to list them. Here, six-year-old JFK made his first public speech at a party honoring his grandfather, John "Honey Fitz" Fitzgerald. JFK announced his bid for Congress at the Parker House, and one night over dinner, he proposed to Jacqueline Bouvier.

60 School St. • Boston, Massachusetts 02108

617-227-8600

www.omnihotels.com/hotels/boston-parker-house

Old City Hall

This Boston monument stands on the site of the original Boston Latin School, the oldest institution of public education in the country. Among its alumni are Cotton Mather, Benjamin Franklin, John Hancock, and Samuel Adams. From this seat of government, John "Honey Fitz" Fitzgerald worked during his two terms as mayor of Boston—the first son of Irish immigrants to win the office.

45 School St. • Boston, MA 02108
617-523-867 • www.oldcityhall.com

Faneuil Hall

Boston's most famous indoor market and political forum, Faneuil Hall has been drawing crowds since 1743. Here Samuel Adams and James Otis urged shoppers and political junkies to support the cause of American independence, and here, in 1979, US Senator Ted Kennedy announced that he would run for the presidency of the United States.

Boston, MA 02109 • 617-523-1300
www.faneuilhallmarketplace.com

St. Stephen's Church

On a summer's day in 1890 the newborn Rose Fitzgerald was carried to this church to be baptized. It is a Boston landmark—the last surviving church designed by renowned Boston architect, Charles Bulfinch. It was built in 1804 for Congregationalists and became a Catholic church after a wave of Irish immigrants moved into the neighborhood and the Yankees moved out.

The church you'll see today does not resemble the church the Fitzgeralds knew when they were parishioners here. Then, the old interior was rich in murals, statues, and other furnishings of a traditional Catholic church. In the late twentieth century, St. Stephen's was returned to the stark look of the building's days as a Congregationalist church.

401 Hanover St. • Boston, MA 02113

617-523-1230 • www.northendboston.com/churches

Rose Fitzgerald Kennedy Greenway

In 2008 the city of Boston, along with several civic and government organizations, came together to open a new string of parks that stretch from the North End, run parallel along a good-sized portion of Boston Harbor, and end in Chinatown. The park was named for one of the city's favorite daughters, Rose Fitzgerald Kennedy. It is a wonderful collection of gardens, promenades, and plazas, accented by sculpture and a very popular carousel.

185 Kneeland St. • Boston, MA 02111

617-292-0020 • www.rosekennedygreenway.org

BOSTON | St. Leonard of Port Maurice Church
4 North Bennet Pl. • Boston, MA 02113
617-726-1191 • saintleonardchurchboston.org

The first thing you'll notice as you reach St. Leonard's is the statuary—the garden leading to the church door is filled with sacred sculptures. But wait until you get inside. Both aisles of the church are crowded with devotional statues of a host of saints.

Around the sanctuary are murals of more saints, while over the altar is a dramatic mural of the apostles looking up in awe as angels carry Our Lady, body and soul, into heaven.

The church's interior decor is exuberant in the style favored throughout Italy—and there is a reason for that. St. Leonard's is the first Catholic parish dedicated to serving immigrants from Italy who were pouring into Boston in the 1870s and the decades that followed.

If you will be in Boston during June and July, check the parish schedule of events—every summer St. Leonard's parishioners sponsor several feasts in honor of their favorite saints. The feasts feature Italian cuisine and music, culminating with a grand procession through the streets in which a large statue of the saint is carried on elaborately decorated platforms.

Consult the parish bulletin on the St. Leonard website for hours of Masses, confessions, and devotions.

STOCKBRIDGE | National Shrine of the Divine Mercy
Eden Hill • Stockbridge, MA 01263
413-298-3931 • www.thedivinemercy.org

Devotion to Jesus Christ under the title "Divine Mercy" is one of the religious phenomena of the late twentieth and early twenty-first centuries. Pope St. John Paul II encouraged Catholics to adopt this devotion, and so strong was his attachment to it that he canonized Sister Faustina Kowalska, who had visions of Jesus and received his messages of the boundless divine mercy he shows to humankind. St. John Paul II also renamed the Sunday after Easter as "Divine Mercy Sunday," linking the message of mercy to the Passion and resurrection of Christ.

Long before any of this, in 1943, Polish Marianist Fathers had settled in Stockbridge, a picturesque New England town in western Massachusetts, where they built a chapel and introduced Catholics of the region to this fledgling devotion. On Eden Hill in Stockbridge, they erected a lovely little chapel with a painting of the Divine Mercy enshrined over the high altar, flanked by beautifully carved and painted statues of the twelve apostles. Above the painting is a marble sculpture of Our Lady the Immaculate Conception—the patroness of the Marianists.

Today, the shrine at Eden Hill covers 350 bucolic acres. The chapel is busy place with daily Masses, confessions, adoration of the Blessed Sacrament, and every day at 3 PM, the recitation of the Chaplet of the Divine Mercy.

On the grounds, you will find many shrines, including a replica of the Grotto at Lourdes and shrines to Mary Mother of Mercy, the

Holy Innocents, and the Holy Family. There are also two groves, one dedicated to St. Thérèse the Little Flower and the other to St. Francis of Assisi, which are reserved as areas of silence for prayer and contemplation.

Every year, the shrine welcomes a Latino pilgrimage that typically draws a crowd of more than five thousand. Other group pilgrimages are welcome, but organizers must call to arrange dates and times for their pilgrimage.

Contact the shrine to learn when it is open to visitors, as well the schedule of Masses, confessions, and devotions to the Divine Mercy.

MICHIGAN

DETROIT | Assumption Grotto
13770 Gratiot Ave. • Detroit, MI 48205
313-372-0762 • www.assumptiongrotto.com

Assumption Grotto—its formal name is Assumption of the Blessed Virgin Mary (Grotto) Parish—is a Detroit parish with a national reputation among Catholics, especially Catholics who promote the Traditional Latin Mass (also known today as the Extraordinary Form). Here the Latin Mass is celebrated daily, along with Masses in English according to the post–Vatican II rite known as the *Novus Ordo,* or Ordinary Form.

The parish began in 1830 when a band of German Catholic immigrants arrived in Detroit just as the city was suffering through an epidemic of cholera. The Germans moved north of the city to a disease-free settlement of French Canadian Catholics (the name of Gratiot Avenue recalls those French settlers). The parish grew and expanded over the decades, until the number of congregants at Assumption was so large that, to meet the needs of its parishioners, the current church was rebuilt and dedicated in 1929.

The lovely Gothic-style white marble high altar has been preserved, along with the communion rail and the many side altars. The parish is a powerhouse of Catholic tradition. The fine art and sublime music—Assumption Grotto Sunday Masses and occasional concerts are renowned across the country—underscore the sacred event taking place at the altar and draws worshippers closer to God.

For a calendar of special events at the Grotto, consult the current bulletin on the parish website, or call or email the Grotto rectory.

Detroit | Ste. Anne de Detroit Church
1000 St Anne St. • Detroit, MI 48216
313-496-1701 • www.ste-anne.org

Two days after Antoine Laumet de la Mothe Cadillac (and, yes, he gave his name to the luxury automobile) came ashore in what is now Michigan with about one hundred French and French Canadian settlers, the colonists founded a church. With their landing just two days before the Feast of St. Anne (Ste. Anne in French), a saint beloved in Old France and New France, the newcomers named their fledgling parish after the mother of the Blessed Virgin Mary and the grandmother of Jesus Christ. This church was built first; the fort to protect the settlers and any displaced Native Americans friendly to the French came later. Since July 26, 1701, there has always been a church of Ste. Anne in Detroit.

By the way, even the name "Detroit" underscores the city's French connection, for it means "the straits," since the Detroit River links Lake Erie and Lake Huron.

During its long history, there have been seven previous churches of Ste. Anne; the one you see today near the International Bridge that connects the United States with Canada was begun in 1886 with the laying of its cornerstone. Many relics and furnishings from the 1818 church were moved into the new Ste. Anne's, and you can see them in the church today. Among these precious historical treasures are: the cornerstone of the 1818 church; in the chapel, the wooden altar where Fr. Gabriel Richard said Mass; the remains of Fr. Richard placed in a contemporary marble shrine; the intricately carved communion rail; the church bell; a statue of St. Anne and her daughter Mary as a young girl; and the oldest stained glass window in Detroit.

The driving force behind the growth of the parish from a frontier outpost to the cathedral of the newly established Diocese of Detroit was Fr. Richard, a French immigrant to the United States who has come to be remembered for his tireless drive to improve conditions in Michigan for all the residents of the territory.

During the War of 1812, the British captured Detroit and insisted that the citizens of the town take an oath of loyalty to the king. Red Reeder records in *The Story of the War of 1812* (Duell, Sloan, and Pearce, 1962) that Fr. Richard refused, saying, "I have taken an oath to support the Constitution of the United States and I cannot take another. Do with me as you please." The British imprisoned the priest, but he was released through the intervention of one of the Native American allies of the British, Chief Tecumseh.

After a fire had devastated Detroit, Fr. Richard arranged for farmers outside Detroit to bring food to the ruined town. He persuaded the federal government to build a road across Michigan. He introduced the first printing press and established the first newspaper. He served in the House of Representatives, and was one of the founders of the University of Michigan. When a Protestant congregation found themselves without a pastor, Fr. Richard agreed to serve them; he avoided controversy by basing his sermons on points of doctrine that Catholics and Protestants shared.

In 1832, an epidemic of cholera swept through Detroit. Fr. Richard worked himself to exhaustion nursing the sick and bringing the last sacraments to the dying. In his weakened state, he contracted the disease himself and died. Before you leave Ste. Anne's, say a prayer at his tomb in the chapel.

The Gothic-style church is rich with sacred images—exquisitely carved altars, and paintings and statues of saints popular with the various ethnic groups that have been served at Ste. Anne's (now that most parishioners are Hispanic, images of Our Lady popular in Latin America have been introduced to the church). The oldest stained glass windows date to 1818 and were designed and hand-crafted in Detroit. True to the parish's origins, French saints are well-represented. On St. Anne's altar is a relic of the saint which is venerated each day of the novena in her honor.

For the schedule of Masses, confessions, and other sacraments, and for the dates of the next St. Anne Novena, consult the parish website.

UPPER PENINSULA | Bishop Frederic Baraga Driving Tour
347 Rock St. • Marquette MI 49855
906-227-9117 • www.dioceseofmarquette.org/baragasites

Venerable Frederic Baraga was a Slovenian priest who emigrated to America to work among the Native American tribes of the Upper Midwest. He came from a well-to-do family and had been trained to be a gentleman, to enjoy all the comforts and cultural sophistication that the Austro-Hungarian empire offered to the upper classes.

He gave all that up, renounced his inheritance, and took up residence in what was still a wilderness. Fr. Baraga worked first among the Ottawa, then relocated to Michigan's Upper Peninsula to live among the Ojibwa. Winters were terrible, yet when he was called upon to bring the sacraments to any member of his flock, he put on his snowshoes and made his way through subfreezing temperatures and deep snowdrifts. In his old age, he put aside his snowshoes and traveled by dog sled. He suffered from isolation—for years Fr. Baraga was the only Catholic priest on the southern shore of Lake Superior—and was often dispirited by the vast, empty country that he had taken as his mission field. Yet, he would not ask his superiors for another assignment, particularly after he was named bishop of Upper Michigan.

While attending a church council in Baltimore, Bishop Baraga suffered a stroke. Even under these circumstances, he insisted on being taken home, rather than remaining in a city where he would have received the finest medical attention and been well cared for in a hospital or a private home. He survived the journey back to the Upper Peninsula, dying in Marquette, Michigan, where you can find his tomb and his shrine.

For information about the sites on this driving tour, including addresses and phone numbers, consult the Baraga page on the Diocese of Marquette website.

Indian Lake Mission Chapel

F r. Baraga was still a novice missionary when he arrived at this spot north of present-day Manistique, Michigan, and found that the Native Americans had begun to build a small church. He helped them complete it, and he dedicated it to the Blessed Virgin Mary.

There is a log cabin chapel at the site, a replica of what the original may have looked like. To continue the frontier appearance of the tiny church, the Stations of the Cross are painted on leather. There is also a small stained glass window of a Native American welcoming Fr. Baraga to Indian Lake. On the grounds is a cemetery with the graves of many of Fr. Baraga's Native American congregation, and a thirty-foot-high copper cross.

8970 County Rd. 442 • Manistique, MI 49854

The Mission at Assinins

A French Canadian settler wrote to Fr. Baraga that Native Americans who had been baptized Catholic or had learned of the Catholic faith often showed up at his door and asked him to read to them from the Bible.

He built a church here dedicated to the Holy Name of Jesus, a school for the Native Americans, and a house for himself. After he had baptized an Ojibwe chief, Assinins, the area was renamed in the chief's honor.

From 1843 to 1853, Assinins was Fr. Baraga's home base from which he set out on his epic journeys through Michigan, Wisconsin, and Minnesota.

Today, the mission, located at Keweenaw Bay on Lake Superior in the Upper Penisula, preserves the schoolhouse where Fr. Baraga taught classes, and the cemetery where you will find the grave of Chief Assinins. There is also on the grounds of a fine sculpture of Venerable Frederic with an Native American warrior and a child.

US Route 41 • Assinins, MI 49908

The Baraga House

This plain house of red sandstone brick was the "bishop's palace" in Marquette. It stands beside St. Peter's Cathedral, and was Bishop Baraga's residence from 1855 until his death in 1868. The house preserves some of the bishop's personal belongings, and you can see the room where he died.

St. Peter Cathedral / Venerable Bishop Baraga Crypt

Bishop Baraga laid the cornerstone of St. Peter's Cathedral in 1866, two years before his death. Two fires compelled the Diocese of Marquette to rebuild its cathedral, each time larger and finer than the one that had been destroyed. The current cathedral was consecrated in 1939. It is a handsome Romanesque-style building, with wonderfully intricate grillwork in the sanctuary, and above the altar is a mural of Christ presenting the keys of heaven to St. Peter.

Beneath the cathedral of St. Peter is a crypt where seven bishops of Marquette lie buried. There is a kneeler before the tomb of Venerable Frederic.

311 W. Baraga Ave. • Marquette, MI 49855

906-226-6548 • www.stpetercathedral.org

Bishop Baraga Shrine

In the early 1970s, L'Anse, Michigan, a French term that means "the end of the bay," was chosen as the site for a monumental shrine to Bishop Baraga. The brass sculpture stands thirty-five feet high. In his right hand, the bishop holds a cross, and in his left hand a pair of snowshoes. Below him are five tepees, representing the missions he founded among the Native American nations. The shrine overlooks Keweenaw Bay, another waterway often navigated by Bishop Baraga.

17570 US Route 41 • L'Anse, MI 49946

(906) 524-7021

MINNESOTA

GRAND MARAIS | St. Francis Xavier Church
(CHIPPEWA CITY CATHOLIC CHURCH)
8 South Broadway • PO Box 1293
Grand Marais, MN 55604 • 218-387-2883
www.cookcountyhistory.org/chippewa_church

From the outside, St. Francis Xavier Church looks like any other simple wooden church in rural America. But inside, you can see that it is a log cabin. Frank Wiskop, a carpenter of the Native American Ojibwa nation, built the  church interior of hand-hewn, dovetailed timber.

It has a homey, pioneer look, and the usual furnishings of a Catholic church—and very few of them are on display so as to prevent the potentially light-fingered from walking off with a valuable artifact—are also low-key: a Mass-produced statue of Our Lady and a colored print of St. Joseph. The altar is a surprise, with columns supporting the altar table, and above it an elegant tablet crowned by pediment, such as you'd find over an ancient Greek or Roman temple, or over the White House and the US Capitol for that matter.

The church was built by Jesuit missionaries to minister to the Ojibwa, but the parish did not last long, only from 1895 until 1936, when the final Mass was offered on Christmas Day. The population of Chippewa City kept dwindling until it became a ghost town. Thanks to the generosity of the Grand Portage Band of Chippewa and the Minnesota Historical Society, St. Francis Xavier Church has survived into a new century.

MINNEAPOLIS | Fr. Hennepin Memorial
Basilica of St. Mary • 1600 Hennepin Ave
Minneapolis, MN 55403 • 612-333-1381
www.mary.org

Decades ago, when school courses on state history were trendy, New York young people learned that Fr. Louis Hennepin was the first European to see Niagara Falls, while those in Minnesota learned that Fr. Hennepin was the first European to see the Falls of St. Anthony at what is now Minneapolis. The New Yorkers never heard about Fr. Hennepin in Minnesota; the Minnesotans never heard about Fr. Hennepin in New York. The cause might have been chauvinism, or perhaps the laser-like focus of the textbook writers. Who knows?

Putting aside the eccentricities of school curricula, it's interesting to learn that in addition to laboring to win souls for Christ, many Catholic missionaries were valiant explorers. French priests charted the St. Lawrence River and the Great Lakes. Jesuit Fr. Jacques Marquette and his fellow explorer, French Canadian Louis Jolliet (also spelled Joliet, as in the name of the city in Illinois), traveled far down the Mississippi River. They had planned to follow it all the way to the Gulf of Mexico, but by this time, the territory that once had been claimed by France was now in the possession of Spain, and the two explorers did not want to risk sitting in a Spanish jail, so they turned back long before they reached their goal.

Fr. Hennepin was a Recollet priest, an order affiliated with the Franciscans. He had two goals in the seventeenth century: to make it easier for future missionaries to find fast, safe routes to the tribes of what is now the American Midwest and to identify potential trade routes for French and Canadians who exchanged European goods for the Native Americans' furs.

To commemorate Fr. Hennepin's journeys of discovery and their impact on the development of Minnesota, in 1940 the Knights of Columbus commissioned a life-sized sculpture of him, which stands on the grounds of St. Mary's Cathedral in Minneapolis. Imbedded into the pedestal is a bas relief of Fr. Hennepin naming the falls in honor of St. Anthony. The relief is based on a painting of the same scene that hangs in the Minnesota State Capitol. By the way, there is also a mural of Fr. Hennepin at Niagara Falls, at the station of the New York Power Authority near the Falls.

St. Paul | Cathedral of St. Paul
238 Selby Ave. • St. Paul, MN 55102
651-228-1766 • www.cathedralsaintpaul.org

The Cathedral of St. Paul in Minnesota enjoys a rare privilege: in 2012 Pope Benedict XVI established "a bond of spiritual affinity" between the St. Paul's of Minnesota and St. Paul Outside the Walls in Rome. This means that pilgrims who pray in the Cathedral of St. Paul gain all the graces and spiritual blessings as if they were praying at the tomb of St. Paul the Apostle in

Rome. To recall this singular event in the history of the cathedral, the Vatican sent a stone from the wall that surrounds the tomb of St. Paul.

The current church was begun in 1904, only forty-six years after the previous Cathedral of St. Paul had been consecrated, with the first Mass held on Palm Sunday 1915. It reveals how quickly the Catholic population of St. Paul was growing that the existing cathedral proved to be too small.

The architects chose a style popular at the time in Europe and the United States, called Beaux arts. It is marked by rich sculptural decoration, broad, soaring arches, and in some cases, a large dome, such as the one that crowns the Cathedral of St. Paul. Other examples of Beaux arts masterpieces are the New York Public Library on Fifth Avenue and Washington, DC's Union Station.

The altar, the heart of every Catholic church, stands beneath a baldacchino, or canopy, supported by six columns of black and gold marble. Resting on the columns is a bronze dome upon which stand statues of St. Paul and two angels.

Around the sanctuary are six chapels dedicated to saints that are the patrons of the ethnic groups that built up the Church in Minneapolis-St. Paul: St. Anthony of Padua for the Italians, St. John the Baptist for the French, St. Patrick for the Irish, St. Boniface for the Germans, Sts. Cyril and Methodius for the Slavs, and St. Thérèse the Little Flower as the patron of all missions.

In the chapel of the Blessed Virgin, you'll find a sculpture of Mary as a young woman, holding the Christ child in her arms. It is an especially lovely work, and the sculptor, Leon Hermant, considered it the finest piece he ever created.

Around the dome are twenty-four stained-glass windows of

angels, and below the windows are mosaics that represent the four cardinal virtues—prudence, temperance, fortitude, and justice. Below the mosaics stand twelve-foot-high sculptures of the four Evangelists.

The stained glass is exceptional. One window in particular is unusual: the north rose window depicts the eight Jesuit martyrs, French members of the Society of Jesus who died for the Faith during the 1600s at the hands of the Iroquois. Canonized in 1930, they were among the first saints of North America, yet one rarely finds paintings, statues, or stained-glass windows of them outside of their shrines in Auriesville, New York, and Midland, Ontario. It is a pleasant surprise to find them honored so prominently in the Cathedral of St. Paul.

For the hours of Mass, confessions, and devotions, to arrange a private tour or join a group tour, and to attend a concert in the cathedral or another special event, consult the parish website.

MISSISSIPPI

Bay St. Louis | St. Augustine Seminary
ST. AUGUSTINE SEMINARY
199 Seminary Dr. • Bay St. Louis, MS 39520 • 228-467-6414
www.svdsouth.com/st.-augustine-seminary.html

St. Augustine's Retreat Center
510 N. 2nd St. • Bay St. Louis, MS 39520 • 228-467-2032

"It must be clear to everyone that it is surely a grave injustice to exclude a whole race from the priesthood, principally because prejudice will greatly hamper them in their religious activities, or a cordial cooperation with white priests may meet with great obstacles," wrote Fr. Matthew Christmann, SVD, according to the parish website. "Such an injustice is bound to work havoc and bring down heavy vengeance upon him who becomes guilty of it."

You can imagine how that statement was met among Catholics and non-Catholics in 1926. And bear in mind that this type of racial prejudice was not limited to the South—it was a pandemic across the United States. By the way, the seminary was named St. Augustine's because this great doctor of the church was an African.

By opening St. Augustine's, the first seminary in the United States founded specifically to train African Americans for the Catholic priesthood, the Divine Word Fathers committed themselves to opposing racism in the Catholic Church and to bringing the faith to African Americans who knew little or nothing about Catholicism. It was a tall order that was tackled by four young African American men who were ordained at St. Augustine's in 1934. Two thousand faithful showed up to witness this extraordinary moment in the history of the Church in the United States.

Today, St. Augustine's operates a retreat center, staffed by members of the Society of the Divine Word. You are welcome to come for a private retreat, join a group retreat or a workshop, or arrange for counseling.

Natchez | St. Mary Basilica
105 S. Union St. • Natchez, MS 39120
601-445-5616 • www.stmarybasilica.org

One of the many joys of visiting Natchez, Mississippi, is exploring on foot the historic district, especially the incredible antebellum mansions that make Scarlett O'Hara's fictional Tara plantation look like a shack. Among the jewels of the historic district is St. Mary Basilica. It is a masterpiece of Gothic Revival architecture, and the interior is nothing short of breathtaking.

Lacy carvings in marble and wood, beautiful statues of the saints everywhere—even on the columns that support the Gothic vaults of the ceiling—exquisite stained glass windows, all but four of them imported from Austria in the 1880s, the beauty of St. Mary draws the heart and soul closer to God.

Over the altar is a painting of the crucifixion, with only Our Lady at the foot of the cross. The point is not to deemphasize the fearless loyalty of St. John, St. Mary Magdalene, and the women disciples who remained with Christ throughout his Passion, but to emphasize the formal title of the basilica—Our Lady of Sorrows.

For times of Mass and confessions, consult the parish website. It may be possible to arrange a tour of St. Mary's—contact the parish well in advance of your visit to inquire.

MISSOURI

FLORISSANT | Old St. Ferdinand Shrine
1 Rue St. Francois • Florissant, MO 63031
314-837-2110 • www.oldstferdinandshrine.com

The church of St. Ferdinand has three patrons: the Sacred Heart of Jesus, St. Ferdinand, and St. John Regis. St. Rose Philippine Duschesne, a sister of the Sacred Heart who was canonized by St. Pope John Paul II in 1988, was a  champion of this parish and resided in the adjacent convent in the early nineteenth century.

Out of respect for this devout woman whose life-long dream was to bring the Native American tribes to Christ, parishioners named their church after the guardian of her order. When authority over this region was transferred from France to Spain, the Spanish authorities renamed the town St. Ferdinand in honor of the thirteenth-century Spanish king. And the name St. John Regis came from a renowned seventeenth-century Jesuit preacher, as the Jesuit fathers had close ties to this church. It can be a little confusing.

The high altar displays a large statue of the Sacred Heart, flanked by smaller statues of St. Ferdinand and St. John Regis. Beneath the altar, behind a glass plate, is a life-size wax sculpture of a priest in the red vestments of a martyr: within the wax are relics of St. Valentine—not the patron saint of lovers whose feast is celebrated on February 14, but another Valentine. (It was a popular name in ancient Rome, and many Valentines appear on the ancient lists of martyrs.) Aside from his name and the fact of his martyrdom, we know nothing else about this early Christian.

Flanking the high altar are two paintings, one of the crucifixion, the other of Our Lady embracing the lifeless body of her son, Jesus. Some sources will tell you that these paintings are the work of the students of the Flemish baroque master, Peter Paul Rubens. The sources are wrong. There is nothing about these paintings that resemble the work of Rubens—there is no drama, no swirling draperies, and the color red—Rubens' favorite—is barely apparent.

Tours of the church and the convent are available at no charge, although a donation is always welcome. Call ahead to make a reservation.

The shrine complex is now in private hands, the Friends of Old St. Ferdinand. It is no longer a parish, but Mass is said in the church from time to time. Call or check the website to learn about the next scheduled Mass.

St. Charles | Shrine of St. Philippine Duchesne
619 N. 2nd St. • St. Charles, MO 63301
636-946-6127 • www.duchesneshrine.org

As a young woman in France, Rose Philippine Duchesne's desire to enter a convent was opposed by her family and frustrated by the French Revolution, which shut down religious houses and often killed the monks and nuns who lived there. After the Revolution, when anti-Catholic sentiment in France diminished somewhat, Rose joined the Religious Sisters of the Sacred Heart.

Over the years, Rose had heard French missionary fathers who had worked among the Native American tribes of the Louisiana Territory talk about their experiences in the American wilderness and the tremendous need for more missionaries—priests and women religious—to bring the faith and education to the Native-American peoples. Rose hoped to go on the American mission, but at the time, the Sacred Heart Sisters had no convent in that far-off country.

That changed in 1817 when Bishop William DuBourg, a refugee from the French Revolution who had been named bishop of Louisiana and Florida, returned home to France to recruit missionaries for his enormous diocese. With the approval of her superior, forty-seven-year-old Rose volunteered, and led four religious sisters to the Louisiana Territory.

The Sacred Heart Sisters began by opening a school in St. Charles. Year after year, Rose's superiors moved her throughout Louisiana and Missouri to open new schools, but they did not send her to the one place where she longed to be—Native American country.

Finally, when she was seventy-two years old, Rose was sent to Kansas to teach the Potawatomi, a Native American people of the Great Plains, upper Mississippi River, and Western Great Lakes region. But she could not learn the language, and so her attempt to teach the Native Americans was an utter failure. After a year in Kansas, her superiors ordered her back to St. Charles, where she died in 1852 at age eighty-two.

Almost at once, Rose was venerated as a saint. Three years after her death, her grave was opened and her body was found to be intact. Her remains were moved to the little octagonal chapel. Today, she rests in a sarcophagus in the shrine church dedicated to her memory.

The exterior of the church is in the Romanesque style, but the inside, designed in the 1960s, is starkly modern; understandably, some pilgrims find the church cold and uninviting. Rose's tomb lies in a tiny side chapel, below an antique crucifix that comes from the Visitation Sisters Monastery of Sainte-Marie-d'en-Haut in Grenoble, France, where she had been a student.

Near the shrine church stands the little brick convent where Rose lived and died. You can visit the parlor and Rose's cell. There is also a museum of some of Rose's meager personal belongings, and some of the uncomfortable-looking furnishings that the Sacred Heart nuns endured in this pioneer outpost.

The shrine is open from 8 AM to 4 PM. Contact the shrine to confirm its hours of operation, and for hours of Mass, other devotions, and guided tours.

St. Louis | Basilica of St. Louis, King of France (the Old Cathedral)
209 Walnut St • St. Louis, MO 63102
314-231-3250 • www.oldcathedralstl.org

The Basilica of St. Louis, King of France, formerly the Cathedral of Saint Louis, and colloquially referred to as the Old Cathedral, is the only example in America of a historic Catholic landmark positioned under a modern secular landmark. The basilica—the oldest Catholic church and the oldest building in St. Louis—stands below the monumental Gateway Arch, a glittering symbol of St. Louis's historic role as the gateway to the American West.

When it was consecrated in 1834, the Old Cathedral was surrounded by homes and businesses. Today, the busy old neighborhood has been replaced by a park that has become the Jefferson National Expansion Memorial, a tribute to President Thomas Jefferson's purchase of the Louisiana Territory from France. (There is a new cathedral, too, outside downtown St. Louis.)

There has been a Catholic church here since 1764, when St. Louis—then known as Laclede's Village—was founded. The Old Cathedral has had a rich history. One of the first chapters of the St. Vincent de Paul Society, an organization of laity that assisted their neighbors in need, was established here. As well, the son of Sacagawea, the guide of explorers Lewis and Clark across the West, was baptized here. Later, after the famous expedition had come home, three of William Clark's children were baptized in the Old Cathedral.

Among St. Louis's art treasures are paintings that Bishop William DuBourg brought back from Europe in 1818. You can find them in the nearby museum. The church was built in the elegant Greek Revival style, and that elegance has been recently restored, especially inside, following an ambitious and successful restoration project. Over the entrance to the cathedral is a Latin inscription that reads, "In honor of St. Louis. Dedicated to the One and Triune God. AD 1834." Above the inscription are the Hebrew characters for the holy name of God.

For opening times and hours of Mass and confession, consult the website.

MONTANA

CROW AGENCY | Myles Keogh Marker, Little Bighorn
Battlefield National Monument
756 Battlefield Tour Rd. • Crow Agency, MT 59022
406-638-2621 • www.nps.gov/libi/index.htm

Most visitors who make the trek out to the Little Bighorn Battlefield come to see Custer's Last Stand, the spot where General George Armstrong Custer and his men fell during a fierce and hopeless battle against Lakota and  Cheyenne warriors. By all means, seek out this famous site, but also look for the white marble marker—much like a headstone—that identifies the place where Captain Myles Keogh was killed.

In 1860 when Blessed Pope Pius IX called for Catholic volunteers to come and fight in defense of the Papal States against the army of Giuseppe Garibaldi, Keogh, then twenty years old, was one of 1,400 Irishmen who left their homeland to fight for the Holy Father. In 1862 Keogh met New York's Archbishop John Hughes, who encouraged him to emigrate to America and fight as an officer in the Union Army. After the Civil War, Keogh continued his career in the US military, and was sent out west, where he was assigned to the famous Seventh Cavalry under General Custer.

It is said that at the Battle of the Little Bighorn, Captain Keogh, then thirty-six years old, was the last cavalryman to die (impossible to know if that tradition is accurate). Three days after the battle, a burial party arrived at the site and interred each soldier where he had fallen. The next year, however, in 1877, some of Keogh's friends in Auburn, New York, paid to have his remains exhumed and reburied in their family plot in Fort Hill Cemetery.

Tickets for a guided tour are available at the Battlefield Visitors Center. Tours operate from Memorial Day through Labor Day, 10 AM to 3 PM. Contact the park service there for current ticket prices.

St. Ignatius | St. Ignatius Mission
300 Bear Track Ave. • St. Ignatius, MT 59865
406-745-2768

It is a tribute to the courage and commitment of European priests and women religious who left their homelands to plant and nourish the Catholic faith in the American wilderness. One of these was Pierre Jean De Smet, a Belgian, who traveled to the United States in 1821. After beginning his studies as a Jesuit in Baltimore, he was sent to Florrisant, Missouri, where he first encountered Native Americans and learned from them some of their customs and the basics of their languages.

About this time the Flathead tribe sent three delegations to the bishop of St. Louis requesting a "black robe" to minister among them. After their fourth visit—bear in mind that it was a journey of 1,500 miles from Flathead country to St. Louis, one way— the bishop sent Fr. De Smet, another Jesuit priest, and two Jesuit brothers to serve the tribes and establish missions among them. One of these was St. Ignatius Mission, founded by Fr. De Smet in 1854.

The current church was built in the early 1890s and decorated by Brother Joseph Carignano, who painted nearly sixty murals on the ceiling, above the high altar, and over the side altars. Brother Carignano was not trained as an artist, but as you'll see, he had natural talent.

There is a museum on-site that displays artifacts made by the local tribes, as well as relics from the mission.

The mission church is open daily during the summer months and often during the winter. Contact the mission for specific dates and times it and the museum are open, and to learn when Mass will be celebrated.

NEBRASKA

OMAHA | Girls and Boys Town National Headquarters
14100 Crawford St. • Boys Town, NE 68010
402-498-1300 • www.boystown.org

I n December 1917, Fr. Edward
Flanagan, a young priest from Ireland,
rented a boarding house and took in boys
who were orphaned or had been abandoned by their families. Fr. Flanagan felt
that the need was especially urgent, as

many of these boys were getting into trouble with the law and were
in danger of going to a reformatory where the older boys would
corrupt them further. His ministry to Omaha's "lost boys" proved
to be a tremendous success, and within a few months, the boarding
house was home to about one hundred.

To relieve the overcrowding, in 1921 Fr. Flanagan, his staff of
School Sisters of Notre Dame and lay volunteers packed up the
boys and relocated to a farm outside Omaha.

The farm eventually became the Village of Boys Town, with a
school, dormitories, and an all-boy village government elected by
the young men themselves. Fr. Flanagan's success with reclaiming
troubled, unwanted boys from the streets brought him international attention. In fact, one day, Hollywood came knocking
on his door. The result was the movie *Boys Town*, starring two
of Hollywood's most popular actors, Spencer Tracy and Mickey
Rooney. Tracy's portrayal of Fr. Flanagan won him an Academy

Award for Best Actor. (Tracy gave the golden Oscar statue to Boys Town.)

In the years after World War II, at the urging of President Harry S Truman, Fr. Flanagan took his mission to Europe. He was still doing what he called "God's work" among orphaned and displaced children when he suffered a fatal heart attack. He was buried at Boys Town's Catholic Dowd Memorial Chapel of the Immaculate Conception. His tomb can be visited there to this day.

In addition to the handsome Gothic-inspired chapel, visitors are welcome to explore the Hall of History, which traces Fr. Flanagan's life as well as the history and evolving mission of Boys Town (now Girls and Boys Town). With classrooms, workshops, a farm, and group homes for the boys and girls, this town is a very busy place. But there is one spot at least where residents, staff, and visitors can escape for a few moments of peaceful contemplation: the Garden of the Bible, a lovely, serene three-acre retreat that features more than 150 flowers, trees, and shrubs mentioned in sacred scripture.

NEVADA

LAS VEGAS | Guardian Angel Cathedral
302 Cathedral Way • Las Vegas, NV 89109
702-735-5241 • www.gaclv.org

Vegas, baby! It's the last place on earth where you'd think that visitors would want to go to Mass and confession and devotions. Yet the cathedral parish staff will tell you that they see a surprising number of out-of-towners at their church.

The cathedral was built in 1963 in the A-frame style that was popular at the time for homes and public buildings. It might not be your favorite architectural design, but no one could mistake Guardian Angel for anything other than a church. And at the cathedral you won't find even a trace of the glitz for which Las Vegas is famous.

The architecture of Guardian Angel is the work of Los Angeles architect Paul R. Williams who, among other landmark buildings, designed the St. Jude Children's Research Hospital in Memphis, Tennessee. The stained glass and mosaics are a collaboration between two Hungarian sisters, Isabel and Edith Piczek. As young women they began to develop a style of sacred art that became known as mystical realism. But behind the Iron Curtain in post–World War II central Europe, the Communist Party would not tolerate anything that was seen as modern, let alone avant garde.

To pursue their careers, the sisters had to leave Hungary and establish themselves in the West.

Isabel and Edith settled in Rome, where in three years they created more than forty murals. From Rome they emigrated to the United States and set up a studio in Los Angeles. They received countless commissions from Catholic parishes in the West, and were invited to create a Massive stained glass entrance way for the Basilica of the National Shrine of the Immaculate Conception in Washington, DC.

The dramatic stained glass windows the sisters created for Guardian Angel are based on the Stations of the Cross. By including figures who were in the news in the 1960s, the sisters gave their windows an extra dimension—they were as much a meditation on the passion of Our Lord as they were a commentary on their times.

Even if you are not a fan of 1960s art and architecture, Williams's design and the Piczeks' works of art may win you over as they underscore the sacred character of Guardian Angel.

For hours of Mass, confessions, and novenas, consult the cathedral website.

NEW HAMPSHIRE

Enfield | Shrine of Our Lady of La Salette

410 NH Route 4A • Enfield, NH 03748

603-632-7087 • www.lasaletteofenfield.org

Enfield Shaker Village

447 NH Route 4A • Enfield, NH 03748

603-632-4346 • www.shakermuseum.org

Over the years, the Catholic Church in America has acquired defunct Protestant churches and converted them for Catholic worship. But Enfield's case is unique: this is the only site in America where what had been a community 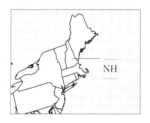 of Shakers was purchased by a Catholic religious order—the Missionaries of La Salette—as a seminary and shrine.

The Shakers were a millenarian sect, known formally as the United Society of Believers in Christ's Second Appearing. They came to America from England in the 1700s. The Shakers were celibate; men and women lived apart. Since they did not produce more Shakers in the typical fashion, they relied upon converts to replenish their communities. They also adopted orphaned children and raised them as Shakers. By the way, their name comes from their unusual method of worship, with the faithful singing and dancing. Although the dances were carefully choreographed, to outsiders it appeared that what the Shakers were doing was awkward, which led to them to be known first as "Shaking Quakers" and then the shortened pejorative term "Shakers."

The Shakers believed that every act they performed, even the least significant, became significant once it was done for love of God. This was a belief the Shakers and St. Thérèse the Little Flower shared, although they never knew of each other. But as a result of this worldview, the ingenuity and high degree of craftsmanship of the Shakers's products, from baskets, to storage boxes, to furniture, have become prized by museums and private collectors.

This Shaker village at Enfield was founded in 1793, and at its peak, in the 1850s was home to three hundred Shaker men, women, and children. The community farmed three thousand acres while also working in their craft shops. The most memorable feature at Enfield is the handsome Great Stone Dwelling, one of the largest buildings the Shakers ever constructed.

By the 1920s, the Shaker community in Enfield was in decline—they simply were not getting new members. Rather than see their property and historic buildings pass to a real-estate developer or some other secular investor, the Shakers sold their property to the La Salette Fathers, who would maintain the spiritual and educational character of the site. After the La Salette Fathers left the property in the 1980s—like the previous owners, the La Salettes were no longer getting the vocations and students necessary to make the place viable—a group of private individuals came together to purchase the grounds and buildings as a museum of Shaker life. Side by side with the Shaker museum is the La Salette Shrine, operated by La Salette Fathers and Brothers.

The shrine has several chapels as well as walking trails with magnificent views of Lake Mascoma and Mount Assurance. The loveliest chapel is the Mary Keene Chapel, built in the Renaissance style and richly furnished. Today, it is part of the museum complex; Mass is said in the La Salette Chapel.

If you would like to make a retreat here, rooms with private baths are available in the historic Great Stone Dwelling. Meals are not served, but this is a rare opportunity to experience one of the architectural gems of New England and revitalize your spiritual life amid the beauty of God's creation.

Call for dates when the shrine and the museum are open to visitors. Consult the shrine website for the hours of Mass. Call or check the website of the museum for dates when it is open and for availability of the accommodations in the Great Stone Dwelling.

NEW JERSEY

NEWARK | Cathedral Basilica of the Sacred Heart
89 Ridge St. • Newark, NJ 07104
973-484-4600 • www.cathedralbasilica.org

For the parishioners of Sacred Heart, it must have seemed a wonder that the Cathedral was ever completed. Almost from the beginning of its building in 1913, rival architects argued over the design of the church. There  were squabbles over whether the church towers could support steeples. And there was even a row about what type of stone to use.

In 1928, the new bishop of Newark, Thomas Walsh, had had enough. Although the cathedral was far from finished, he opened it for public worship. The great church was not dedicated until 1954, forty-one years after the first plans for the cathedral were prepared. That's something of a record—so many American cathedrals were built in much less time.

It was worth the wait. Sacred Heart is glorious, inside and out. The first architects were inspired by the great medieval Gothic cathedrals of France, such as Chartres and Rouen. Around and over the portals are fine sculptures, bas reliefs; magnificent bronze doors lead worshippers inside the church. Once across the vestibule, you'll find an incredibly complex Gothic-style screen that draws you into the main body of the church.

Along the walls of the side aisles are the fourteen Stations of the Cross in mosaic, set in elaborately carved frames and installed above small altars. The carvings of the baptismal font and the pulpit are exquisite, as is the baldachino or canopy that soars above the altar which bears a strong resemblance to the baldachino in St. Patrick's Cathedral in New York City.

Around the sanctuary are side chapels dedicated to eight saints. And everywhere you look there are splendid stained glass windows of scenes from sacred scripture and from the lives of a host of saints beloved by the people of the Diocese of Newark.

Sacred Heart is so glorious that it defies description. Make an effort to visit this cathedral and discover for yourself the exceptional beauty of this holy place.

SUMMIT | Dominican Monastery of Our Lady of the Rosary
543 Springfield Ave. • Summit, NJ 07901
908-273-1228 • www.summitdominicans.org

The Dominican nuns here support themselves in a way that is out of the ordinary. They make soap, specifically scented soap; candles, both scented and unscented; lip balm; and for guys, a shaving set that includes a brush made of real boar bristles, a stoneware shaving mug, and balls of shaving soap. And, as point of fact, they do a thriving business.

The Dominicans have been in Summit, New Jersey, since 1939, but the monastery they envisioned for themselves was never realized, in part due to the Great Depression and America's entry into World War II. Now, with more and more young women asking to be admitted to the community, and with the growth of the soap-and-candle-making business, it is more imperative than ever that a new wing be added to the existing monastery for nuns' cells and an expanded workshop, not to mention more parking for the ever-increasing number of pilgrims who come to the monastery chapel, and new facilities to make the monastery accessible to the disabled. The cost has been estimated at $4 million, and the community hopes to have it completed in 2019, in time for their eighth anniversary.

The monastery's chapel doors are opened each day at 6 AM, and visitors come to adore the Blessed Sacrament, attend Mass, or perhaps to listen as the sisters pray the Divine Office. The doors are shut at 7 PM.

The chapel is lovely, with a carved wooden screen separating the nuns' choir from the body of the chapel, where visitors fill the pews. After spending time with Our Lord in the chapel, most visitors make their way to the gift shop—call for the shop's hours of operation. You'll find the sisters' products hard to resist, and every purchase helps support them and move them a step closer to their expanded monastery.

NEW MEXICO

ABIQUIU | Monastery of Christ in the Desert
PO Box 270 • Abiquiu, NM 87510
575-613-4232, 575-613-4274
www.christdesert.org

Like the very first Christian monasteries founded in the deserts of Egypt more than 1,700 years ago, it's not easy to get to the Monastery of Christ in the Desert. This magnificent Benedictine house of prayer is set in the Chama Canyon, at the foot of a high bluff, and stands at the end of approximately fifteen miles of unpaved road—to get to Christ in the Desert you'll be better served using a four-wheel-drive vehicle. Granted, it takes some effort to reach the monastery, but the location guarantees that here you will experience the profound silence that is essential for an intimate communion with God.

The monastery's architecture—the work of architect George Nakashima—is a masterpiece: it will probably remind you of traditional Pueblo architecture, and even the mysterious cities of the ancient cliff-dwelling tribes of the American Southwest.

In his Rule—the model for all subsequent monastic rules in the West—St. Benedict instructed his monks, "Let all guests who arrive be received as Christ." And so day visitors, as well as those making a retreat at the monastery, are welcome at Christ in the Desert.

Guests are invited to join the monks in their life of prayer, which begins at 4:00 AM and concludes at 7:30 PM. The motto of the Benedictine community is *ora et labora* ("prayer and work"), and the monks hope their guests will join them in the day-to-day tasks necessary for the upkeep of the monastery.

The setting of Christ in the Desert is so spectacular that you will be drawn to explore the area, but remember that you are in the wilderness, so be ruled by common sense. The mesas behind the monastery can be dangerous, especially to novice climbers. If you want to go hiking, discuss the matter with the guest master—he can recommend the best and safest routes based on your fitness level and experience.

The monastery is beautiful. The church, dedicated to St. John the Baptist, a cousin of Jesus Christ and the model of Christian monasticism (he lived in the desert near the river Jordan) is constructed of a harmonious blend of adobe brick, stone, and wood. Large plate glass windows flood the chapel with natural light. Another highlight of the monastery is the cloister, built around a lovely garden with a fountain in the center. Water gurgles up through the fountain via a solar-powered water system. In fact, Christ in the Desert has adopted many solar-powered initiatives, making it one of the greenest monastic communities in the United States. The monks are also careful to preserve the biodiversity of the surrounding area, including nearby watersheds and wetlands.

To make a reservation for a retreat—and reservations are necessary—consult the monastery website.

Chimayo | El Santuario de Chimayo
15 Santuario Dr. • Chimayo, NM 87522
505-351-9961 • www.holychimayo.us

Unless you've traveled to Latin America, where such intensely personal shrines are fairly common, it's not going too far to say that El Santuario de Chimayo—the Sanctuary of Chimayo—is unlike any other Catholic shrine in the United States.

The origins of the shrine, set about thirty miles north of Sante Fe, New Mexico, are a bit hazy, but most historians believe that it was founded in about 1813 by Bernardo Abeyta, a *penitente*, a member of a religious organization especially devoted to the Passion of Jesus Christ. *Penitentes* perform acts of penance that punish their bodies in order to atone for their sins.

While performing a penitential exercise in the hills of Chimayo, Abeyta discovered a wooden crucifix, skillfully carved and colorfully painted. It reminded him of a similar crucifix venerated in Guatemala, known as Our Lord of Esquipulas, and for that reason, you may hear the crucifix referred to by that title. How Abeyta in New Mexico learned of this Guatemalan devotion is another of the mysteries of this shrine. In any case, with the blessing of the local clergy, he erected a chapel on the spot where he found the crucifix and set up the cross over the altar.

As the number of pilgrims to the chapel increased, a larger chapel was constructed—the one you see today. The interior was adorned with paintings and wooden sculptures of Christ, the Blessed Mother, and a variety of saints. The artists who created these images were not classically trained at any art school, yet the works they produced possess a spiritual quality that is profoundly moving.

To the side of the altar is a little room where you'll find a small pit in the ground. This is the spot where Abeyta found the crucifix more than two hundred years ago. The soil is considered *tierra bendita* (blessed earth), which is said to have healing power; most pilgrims and visitors carry away some of it. Some historians have suggested that the pit was once a mineral spring that Native Americans believed had healing properties, and this tradition was adopted and "baptized" when Catholics settled the region.

A short walk from the Santuario is another chapel dedicated to Santo Nino de Atocha, the Holy Child of Atocha. Inside is a sculpture of the child Jesus, dressed as a medieval pilgrim. According to a pious legend, in the thirteenth century, the Moors captured the town of Atocha in Spain and imprisoned all of the men. The caliph decreed that the prisoners' families were responsible for bringing them food and water, but that only children under the age of twelve would be admitted into the prison. Prisoners who had no children under twelve or whose families were too poor to buy extra food faced starvation.

Then, a little boy began to appear at the prison every day, handing out water and loaves of bread. The women of the town, who had implored Our Lady to spare their men, believed that Mary had answered their prayers and sent her son with food and drink to save the starving prisoners. This chapel then recalls that tradition.

Open daily 9 AM to 5 PM from October through April, and 9 AM to 6 PM from May through September.

Consult the website or call for times of Mass and confession.

RANCHO DE TAOS | San Francisco de Asis Mission
60 St. Francis Plaza • Rancho de Taos, NM 87557
575-758-2754
www.nps.gov/nr/travel/american_latino_heritage/
San_Francisco_de_Assisi_Mission_Church.html

It's not uncommon for parishioners to gather after winter is over to clean up the grounds of their church and plant flowers. But the parishioners of the San Francisco de Asis Mission in Rancho de Taos have a unique annual maintenance tradition: every June they gather with other volunteers to re-mud their adobe church. It has to be done—the weather erodes the dried mud of the church's walls so quickly that if it weren't for a good annual re-mudding, the mission would melt away.

The area around the Taos Pueblo was founded in the 1770s by settlers, most of them farmers, from Mexico and Spain. When speaking of churches, typically we talk about architects and design. But the mission church was sculpted. There is nothing Gothic or baroque or even classically Spanish—whitewashed walls and a red tile roof—such as you find at the string of missions along the coast of California.

San Francisco de Asis looks like it grew out of the ground, and for decades, that natural, organic look has drawn visitors and artists to this enchanting town in northern New Mexico, which is about an eighty-minute drive from Santa Fe. Among the renowned artists who admired, even loved the church, were photographer Ansel Adams and especially painter Georgia O'Keeffe. She returned time and again to paint the church from a variety of angles and at different hours of the day, when the sunlight plays off the oddly shaped buttresses, casting dramatic shadows.

The interior of the church is also a treasure. There are two altars, one with several paintings probably imported from Mexico and a second with folk-art style paintings of saints and a wooden sculpture of the crucifixion in the *santos* style of Latino and Native American artists.

At one time, the church displayed an eighteenth-century painting, entitled *The Shadow of the Cross* by Henri Ault. At the end of the day, when the lights in the church were extinguished, the painting gave off an unearthly glow. The "Mystery Painting," as it has come to be known, has been moved to a dark, climate-controlled environment where visitors can see it and its strange special effects without fear of damaging Ault's enigmatic creation.

The hours the church is open and the time for Mass and confession varies from season to season, so call or check the mission website in advance.

Santa Fe | La Conquistadora Chapel
Cathedral Basilica of Santa Fe
131 Cathedral Pl. • Santa Fe, NM 87501
505-982-5619 • www.cbsfa.org

In 1598, the first Spanish settlers, soldiers, and Franciscan missionary priests arrived in what is now Santa Fe. The soldiers and settlers founded a town, established farms, and traded with the Pueblo Indians who lived in the area. The Franciscans, assisted by the colonists, erected a chapel and began to teach the faith to the

Pueblos. But officials of the Spanish government in Santa Fe were not so benevolent. They enslaved the Native Americans, and mutilated Pueblo men and teenage boys who resisted them.

In 1625 the mission church received an especially fine gift—a sculpture from Spain of the Virgin and Child. It is the oldest statue of Mary and the Infant Jesus in the United States.

The sacred image was venerated in the mission church until 1680, when the Pueblos, led by a warrior named Po-pay, rose up against the Spanish, killing four hundred men, women, and children, including twenty-one Franciscans. Spanish towns, farms, and missions were burned, and Spaniards who managed to get away fled south. The colonists from Santa Fe took with them their prized statue of Our Lady.

More than a decade later, a commander named Don Diego de Vargas was sent into New Mexico to reclaim the territory for Spain. He brought with him the statue of the Virgin and Child. Once Vargas had made peace with Pueblos, Our Lady was venerated in Santa Fe under a new title, "La Conquistadora," (the Conqueror). Today, she is still known in Spanish as La Conquistadora, but in English, as the less warlike Our Lady of Peace.

The statue is enshrined in a chapel behind the high altar of the Cathedral of Santa Fe. The chapel is all that survives of the adobe church that once stood on this site. There is a confraternity at the cathedral that cares for the elaborate robes, veils, and jewels that are the statue's wardrobe. Every summer, La Conquistadora is carried in procession through the streets around the cathedral.

For the times of Mass and confessions, and for a calendar of events, consult the cathedral website.

NEW YORK

AURIESVILLE | Shrine of Our Lady of the Martyrs
136 Shrine Rd., Ste. 2 • Auriesville, NY 12016
518-853-3033 • www.auriesvilleshrine.com

If any place in the United States is holy ground, it is a hilltop shrine in the Mohawk Valley.

Here, one Jesuit priest and two lay missionaries were martyred: St. Isaac Jogues, St. John de La Lande, and St. Rene Goupil. About twenty years after their sacrifice, the Catholic Church's first Native American saint, St. Kateri Tekakwitha, was born to a Mohawk warrior and a captive Algonquin Christian woman. Archeological excavations have shown that the shrine is located on the site of the Mohawk village of Ossernenon, where Fr. Jogues, de La Lande, and Goupil were killed and Tekakwitha was born.

The location, about forty miles from Albany, is lovely, and surprisingly peaceful. Although a major highway runs along the base of the hill, at the shrine the sound of traffic is rarely louder than a faint hum.

The layout and decoration of the shrine is unpredictable, and it has something for everyone. The main church was built in 1930 in tribute to the canonization that year to the three martyred there and also five Jesuit priests martyred in Canada in the 1640s. The shrine was built in the round, reminding the pilgrim of the

Colosseum in Rome where it is believed that many early Christians were martyred for the Catholic faith.

At its center stands a circle of several linked altars, each set against a wall of log palisades, such as protected Native American villages and then European settlements in the valley. The altars are adorned with finely carved and painted statues of saints, including, of course, the saints connected with Ossernenon.

Among the shrine's historic sites, two are especially moving: the site of the torture platform where Jogues and Rene Goupil endured days of agony—the site is marked by a large crucifix; and the Ravine, where St. Rene's body was dumped by the Mohawks after one of the warriors had killed him. Along the path leading down to the stream at the bottom of the Ravine are plaques bearing excerpts from Jogues' memoirs of Goupil's martyrdom and Jogues's attempt to hide the body.

There are many statues on the grounds, including the Sacred Heart, Our Lady under various titles, St. Joseph and other saints. There is also a striking outdoor Stations of the Cross and a series of sculptures of the Seven Sorrows of the Blessed Virgin Mary.

Of the several chapels at the shrine, the St. Kateri Chapel is a standout. Built in 1894 in a log cabin style, it enshrines the Blessed Sacrament and sacred relics, including a relic of Father St. Jean de Brébeuf, who was martyred in Canada in 1649.

For the schedule of Masses, consult the website. For hours of operation, call the shrine.

FONDA | National St. Kateri Tekakwitha Shrine
3628 State Highway 5 • Fonda, NY 12068
518-853-3646 • www.katerishrine.com

At age ten, Tekakwitha (Kateri—Catherine—was the name she would take at her baptism), along with the rest of the people of her village, moved from Ossernenon to a place they called Caughnawaga, near the present-day town of Fonda, New York, about forty-five miles west of Albany.

Nine years later, in 1675, a Jesuit missionary, Fr. Jacques de Lamberville, arrived in the village. While the Jesuits had enjoyed tremendous success converting the Hurons, the Mohawks did not welcome the priests. Fr. de Lamberville made only one convert at Caughnawaga—Kateri, whom he baptized on Easter 1676.

Kateri's conversion outraged her family and her neighbors. They kicked her, beat her, and on one occasion, a Mohawk warrior charged at her with hatchet raised as if he was about to kill, but at the last moment he lowered his weapon and left her in peace.

With Kateri's life in danger, Fr. de Lamberville urged her to travel north about 350 miles to Kahnawake, a village of Christian Native Americans just south of present-day Montreal. Here, safe among like-minded Native Americans, she settled into a routine of prayer and good works that included, typically, attending Mass twice a day, spending time before the Blessed Sacrament, teaching the basics of the faith to small children, and caring for the sick and the elderly.

Almost immediately after her death in 1680, the Jesuit priests at the mission, French settlers, and the Christian Native Americans began to hold Kateri in special veneration. In 2012, Pope Benedict XVI canonized Kateri, the first Native American from the United States to join the vast company of those recognized as saints.

In 1938 a Conventual Franciscan friar, Fr. Thomas Grassman, a man who was part archaeologist, part champion of Kateri, discovered and excavated the site at Caughnawaga and erected a shrine chapel to Kateri in a 200-year-old barn. The site of the village where Kateri was converted and baptized can be found atop a hill above the shrine. The upper level of the barn is the chapel, the lower level is a museum of Native American artifacts, many of them from the Mohawks and the other tribes who comprised the six-nation Iroquois Confederacy.

The barn chapel is simple and rustic, with a painting of St. Kateri over the altar. The shrine also possesses a relic of the saint.

The shrine is open only during the warm weather months. Special events are held at the shrine during the summer, culminating with the Feast of St. Kateri, celebrated for several days around July 14. Check the shrine website for dates and times of special events and hours of operation.

GRAYMOOR AND GARRISON | Franciscan Friars of the Atonement
1350 Route 9 • Graymoor, NY 10524
845-424-3671 • www.atonementfriars.org
FRANCISCAN SISTERS OF THE ATONEMENT
41 Old Highland Turnpike • Garrison, NY 10524
844-437-6287 • www.graymoor.org

To be honest, Graymoor is a bit off the beaten path: it is two to three hours north of Manhattan in an area that is still mostly forest. The closest town is Garrison, New York. The friars and the sisters occupy a high hill, and from the summit, there are wonderful views of the countryside, with the Hudson River in the distance. During the fall, when the trees are aflame with color, the view is magnificent.

In 1898, Fr. Paul Wattson and Mother Lurana White founded a new religious community at Graymoor. Fr. Paul and Mother Lurana were Episcopalians, and they made it their vocation to bring about the reunion of the Anglican/Episcopal Church with the Roman Catholic Church. To set the example, the founders, along with all their friars and sisters, collectively were received into the Catholic Church by Pope St. Pius X.

The sisters live at the bottom of the hill, just off the road. The entrance to Graymoor is easy to spot—watch for the life-size, full-color crucifix. The sisters's complex includes a charming collection of cream-colored stucco buildings, the old chapel, and a stone shrine where a statue of Our Lady of the Atonement is venerated. The chapel is usually locked. But stop by the gift shop—one of the sisters may open it for you if she is not too busy. A modern building is the sisters's current residence.

Up the hill is the friars's residence, also built in a stark modern style. Keep walking up the hill to the old Chapel of St. Francis where, in the early days of the community, the friars celebrated Mass and gathered in the choir for the Divine Office.

The chapel is small, intimate, and beautifully decorated. It has the feel of an old church in rural England, which makes sense, given the friars's and sisters's Anglican roots. At the very top of the hill stands a reproduction of Michaelangelo's Pieta, and directly in front of the sculpture is Fr. Paul's grave. Also on the hilltop is a chapel for Eastern Rite Catholics. Inside you'll find a small collection of antique icons (use the flashlight app on your smartphone, because the interior tends to be dark).

A bit further down the hill stands a large church to accommodate groups of pilgrims. It is built in the style of Quonset hut, but if the exterior is off-putting, the interior can make you forget the utilitarian architecture. The many windows fill the sanctuary with light, and sacred images remind you that are you are indeed in a church.

The friars and the sisters still have an ecumenical outreach program. A high point of their calendar is the annual Week of Prayer for Christian Unity, a tradition at Graymoor established by Fr. Paul in 1908, and subsequently adopted by the Catholic Church in America. Consult the websites for calendars of events, as well as the schedules of daily Masses and morning and evening prayers.

Both the friars and the sisters conduct retreats. For a schedule of upcoming retreats, visit their websites. Remember to make your reservation early and to inquire what donation the friars or sisters ask of their guests.

Finally, maintaining a tradition that dates back to the founding of Graymoor, the friars operate St. Christopher House, a rehab facility for men trying to recover from addictions to narcotics or alcohol. This residence is closed to pilgrims.

LACKAWANNA | Basilica and National Shrine of
Our Lady of Victory
767 Ridge Rd. • Lackawanna, New York 14218
716-828-9444 • www.ourladyofvictory.org

Fr. Nelson Baker was America's St. Vincent de Paul. Like the seventeenth-century French priest, Fr. Baker could never turn away someone in need, and so he spent his sixty years as a parish priest in a city just south of Buffalo, New York, building up the community's existing charitable institutions and founding new ones to meet new needs.

At the time of his death in 1936, Fr. Baker supervised an orphanage, a home for young boys who were, according to one source, "inclined to truancy and willfulness," a home for teenage boys and young men who had just entered the workforce, a residence that offered prenatal care for single mothers, a full-service hospital, and the Association of Our Lady of Victory to fund his many projects.

From his early days as a priest, Fr. Baker had been devoted to the Blessed Mother under her title, Our Lady of Victory. In all of his ambitious undertakings, he relied on her intercession. In 1921, to pay tribute to the many graces he had received through Mary, Fr. Baker, when he was seventy-nine years old, announced that he wanted to build a grand church dedicated to Our Lady of Victory.

Once he sent out his appeal for funds for the shrine, the association office was flooded with contributions—so much so that the church was completed in only five years, and Fr. Baker paid for the construction and decoration of the church—all $3.2 million of it—in cash. He celebrated the fiftieth anniversary of his ordination in the new church. A few months later, Pope Pius XI designated the Church of Our Lady of Victory a minor basilica.

The basilica is grand beyond description, built almost entirely of marble, inside and out, and crowned by a Massive dome only slightly smaller than the dome of the US Capitol in Washington, DC.

The interior is breathtaking, as richly decorated with works of art as any church in Europe. Above the white marble high altar is a nine-foot-tall sculpture of Our Lady of Victory. On the ceiling high above the congregation are five murals inspired by titles from the Litany of Blessed Virgin, showing Mary as Queen of the Angels, Queen of Patriarchs, Queen of Prophets, Queen of Apostles, and Queen of Martyrs. At the center of the dome are murals of Mary's Assumption and her Coronation as Queen of Heaven. Around the edge of the dome are paintings of archangels and apostles.

The figures in the fourteen Stations of the Cross are life-size and powerfully moving. Fr. Baker's favorite is said to have been the fourth station, "Jesus Meets His Afflicted Mother." If he couldn't be found anywhere else, he was most likely here, meditating on this tender scene.

As is true of most grand churches, the basilica has many splendid side altars as well as luminous stained glass windows. And Fr. Baker is here, too. Since 1999, the year the cause that may lead to his canonization began, Fr. Baker's remains have been enshrined in a black marble sarcophagus in the basilica's Chapel of Our Lady of Lourdes.

The basilica is open daily from 7:00 AM to 8:30 PM. For a guided tour of the basilica, contact the office.

NEW YORK CITY | Al Smith Walking Tour

Alfred Emanuel Smith, a four-time governor of New York State, was the first American Catholic nominated for the presidency. He ran on the Democrats' ticket, and after a campaign marred by virulent anti-Catholic rhetoric, lost in a landslide to his Republican rival, Herbert Hoover.

It is no exaggeration to say that the son of a poor, working-class, devoutly Catholic family grew up on the sidewalks of New York. His parents' apartment stood at 174 South Street, a bit south from where the Brooklyn Bridge was being built. (Smith liked to say that he and the bridge grew up together.)

The home Smith and his parents knew in the 1870s is long gone, but there are other Smith-related Lower East Side sites nearby that have survived.

Perhaps more to the point, the atmosphere of this old neighborhood has barely changed since Smith's day. Yes, the residents today are overwhelmingly Chinese rather than Irish, but the teeming streets, the tiny shops that cater to a host of day-to-day necessities, and the heavy traffic are qualities that Smith would recognize.

St. James Church

No surviving record tells us who designed this handsome neo-classical church with the elegant Doric columns that flank the main entrance. The Greek-Revival church, completed in 1836, was the parish of Smith's mother and father, and then of Smith, his wife, Catherine, and their children. Al served as an altar boy at St. James and later joined the parish's amateur theater company.

In the 1870s, the parish books showed that twenty-five thousand Catholics were regular worshippers at St. James, which was typical in over-crowded neighborhoods at the time. The church is especially significant in the history of Irish New York—in 1836 the Ancient Order of Hibernians was founded here to protect Catholic churches and institutions, as well as Catholic clergy, religious, and lay faithful, from anti-Catholic mobs such as the one that had recently burned to the ground, St. Mary's Church on Grand Street.

Sadly, St. James closed its doors in 2014. It is open upon request for weddings, funerals, and special occasions, but otherwise the church is shuttered.

32 James St. • New York, NY 10038

St. James School

This is the only school Smith ever attended. In his day, the 650 boys registered in the school were taught by the Christian Brothers, and the 800 girls by the Sisters of Charity.

In 1886, Smith's father died. He had barely been able to support himself, his wife, and their two children. With his death, the Smiths were nearly penniless. As a result, Al Smith quit school and took a job peddling newspapers on the street until he got a better job at the Fulton Fish Market.

The school, which was founded in 1832, continues to serve the new immigrant families, now under the name of the Transfiguration School.

37 St. James Pl. • New York, NY 10038

www.transfigurationschoolnyc.org

Fulton Fish Market

In the late nineteenth century, the Fulton Fish Market, along the East River south of the Brooklyn Bridge, was one of the major wholesale fish markets in the United States.

Fourteen-year-old Al Smith worked from 4 AM to 4 PM, at a wage of about $12 a week, a respectable wage at the time. And the job had one serious perk—he got to take free fish home to his mother.

During the time he worked at the market, the Smith family lived almost entirely on fish.

In 2005, after 183 years on the same site, the market moved to the Hunts Point section of the Bronx. Today, the site of the old market is a gentrified neighborhood of shops, restaurants, and bars.

Fulton Street • New York, NY

Alfred E. Smith House

Smith, his wife Catherine, and their five children lived in this plain, three-story, red-brick townhouse from 1909 to 1923. Unlike their previous apartment, a cramped third floor walk-up, the Smith family had the entire house to themselves—a real luxury in this neighborhood, even today.

25 Oliver St. • New York, NY 10038

Governor Alfred E. Smith Memorial

A two-minute walk south from the Smith family's house stands the Governor Alfred E. Smith Memorial in the Alfred E.

Smith Playground. This life-size bronze sculpture is the work of Charles Keck, who also sculpted the statue of World War I chaplain Fr. Francis Duffy that stands in Times Square and the commemorative tablet that you'll find on the rear of the dramatic Maine Monument in Columbus Circle.

The sculpture is very fine, but it doesn't quite capture the personality of this gregarious Irish politician, who got such out a kick out of his career that he was nicknamed "The Happy Warrior." Still, Keck has lightened the dignified mood of Smith by including on the podium the derby hat that was Smith's trademark headgear, as well as a sculpture inspired by the popular song "The Sidewalks of New York," which was Smith campaign theme song.

Alfred E. Smith Playground • 76 Catherine St.

New York, NY 10038

www.nycgovparks.org/parks/alfred-e-smith-playground/
monuments/1455

NEW YORK CITY | The Cloisters Museum and Gardens
99 Margaret Corbin Dr. • Fort Tryon Park
New York, NY 10040 • 212-923-3700
www.metmuseum.org/visit/visit-the-cloisters

Rising above the greenery of Fort Tryon Park, nearly at the northernmost tip of Manhattan, stands what appears to be a medieval monastery lifted right out of Catholic Europe. And if that is your first impression, you're not entirely incorrect, because the Cloisters Museum, a branch of New York's Metropolitan Museum of Art, incorporates rooms, chapels, portals, columns, and, of course, cloisters, from several medieval French and Spanish churches and monasteries that, back in their homelands, were falling into ruin.

The founder of this collection of architectural treasures was George Grey Barnard, an American sculptor who spent part of his life living in France. When he came home, he displayed his medieval art collection in his house in northern Manhattan, close to where the Cloisters stands today. In the 1920s he put his collection on the market, and the oil baron, John D. Rockefeller Jr., snapped it up and donated it to the Metropolitan Museum of Art, along with about forty medieval sculptures from his own collection, and a sizable chunk of New York undeveloped real estate that became Fort Tryon Park. Rockefeller marked a hilltop in the soon-to-be park as the site of a one-of-a-kind art museum.

It took four years to build the Cloisters, following the design of architect Charles Collens, who designed New York's medieval-style Riverside Church. Collens's plan called for a museum that incorporated the architectural fragments Barnard had collected, as well as rooms and chambers—rather than traditional art museum galleries—built in the Romanesque and Gothic styles that dominated European architecture in the twelfth to the fifteenth centuries. These rooms were filled with medieval paintings, sculptures, tapestries, stained-glass windows, and precious liturgical vessels and vestments—all of them created by masters during the Middle Ages.

Among the glories of the Cloisters are:

- The Fuentiduena Chapel, from a twelfth-century Romanesque church in Spain. Above the altar is a large fresco of the Virgin and Child, flanked by the archangels St. Michael and St. Gabriel, with the magi, or the three kings, approaching to adore the Christ Child.

- A richly detailed wooden sculpture of three saints by Tilman Riemanschneider, one of the finest sculptors of late medieval Germany.

- Robert Campin's luminous triptych of the Annunciation, with the donors depicted kneeling in prayer in one side panel and St. Joseph shown laboring in his carpentry shop in the other.

- The magnificent Unicorn Tapestries, a series of seven tapestries woven in or near Brussels, Belgium, around 1500. Take some time to study these masterpieces of the weaver's art—the details of animals, plants, and the range of emotions in human facial expressions are incredible.

Some works in the collection are so fragile that they cannot be put on view full time. Among the Cloisters's greatest treasures are a walrus ivory cross made in 1148 for the Abbey of Bury St. Edmunds in England, and the Antioch Chalice, a large silver chalice made in Syria in the sixth century that depicts Christ seated among grape vines that swirl all around the surface of the cup.

And do not miss the various cloisters, each lovely in its own way. A great favorite with visitors is the Bonnefort Cloister, where the museum's gardeners tend plantings of flowers and herbs that were popular in abbey gardens during the Middle Ages. From this cloister garden are the best views of the Hudson and of the soaring cliffs known as the Palisades across the river in New Jersey.

The Cloisters is open daily from 10:00 AM until 5:15 PM (4:45 PM from November through February). The museum is closed on Thanksgiving Day, Christmas Day, and New Year's Day.

New York City | Basilica of St. Patrick's Old Cathedral
263 Mulberry St. (corner of Prince and Mott streets)
New York, NY 10012 • 212-226-8075
www.oldcathedral.org

Old St. Patrick's is one of the overlooked gems of New York City—even many native Catholic New Yorkers are surprised to learn that there is another St. Patrick's Cathedral far south of the grand Gothic church on Fifth Avenue. You'll find it behind a tall brick wall in Little Italy.

When construction of the cathedral was completed in 1815, it was one of only two Catholic churches in Manhattan, one of only three in New York State, and the largest Catholic church in the United States. It was also far from the main population center of Manhattan, which was still confined almost entirely below Canal Street. But the bishops of New York, like New York's real estate investors, knew that as the city grew, it would have to move north, and St. Patrick's would be waiting to serve them.

Old St. Patrick's is interesting even before you step onto the cathedral grounds. All around it is a tall red brick wall, erected to protect the church from rampaging Know Nothings, a rabidly anti-Catholic political party that, in the 1840s and 1850s, targeted Catholic institutions, businesses, and even private homes. Behind the wall is the cemetery, where the Catholic faithful of New York have been buried for more than two hundred years.

In the vestibule, you'll find the cathedral's two oldest stained-glass windows—one of St. Patrick, the other of the Virgin and Child. Mounted on the wall is a large stone tablet that commemorates the Irish Brigade, the incredibly valiant unit that fought in the Civil War (in four years of war, the Irish took approximately four thousand casualties—the highest casualty rate of any brigade in the Union army). In April 1861, in a ceremony at the cathedral, Archbishop John Hughes blessed the banners of the Irish Brigade. Many of the Irishmen marching off to war were members of the parish.

In the main body of the cathedral, you'll find statues of the Sacred Heart, Our Lady, and a host of saints arranged up one aisle and down the other, all with ranks of candles before them.

Behind the altar is a richly carved wooden screen supporting wooden sculptures of the twelve apostles. In the center is a large painting of the Resurrection of Christ, the work of New York artist Frank Herbert Mason.

Since the old cathedral is off the typical tourist trail and its significance unknown to most New Yorkers, it does not see many visitors. On your visit to Old St. Patrick's, you may have the place all to yourself. But the neighborhood has changed—it's become trendy, attracting posh boutiques, hip restaurants and bars, and successful singles, couples, and families, all of which has raised the hopes of the old cathedral's clergy that new members to the parish will make the old church a busy place once again.

For Mass times and a schedule of sacraments and other church services, consult the cathedral website.

NEW YORK CITY | St. Patrick's Cathedral
Fifth Avenue and East 50th Street

The first thing you'll notice when you visit St. Patrick's Cathedral is the throng of people who fill the church. There is a never-ending stream of tourists and casual visitors winding up one side aisle and down the other, snapping photographs, and straining their necks to study the stained glass.

But there are also worshippers—and there are a lot of them—attending one of the daily Masses, lighting candles before the cathedral's innumerable shrines, kneeling in silent prayer before the Blessed Sacrament exposed in the exquisite Lady's Chapel. While cathedrals in other major American cities tend to be quiet places on workdays, St. Patrick's, day after day from opening until closing time, packs them in. Each year, approximately five million visitors come to this glorious Gothic church in the heart of midtown Manhattan. If you've ever stepped inside St. Patrick's when it is decorated for Christmas, it can seem as if all five million have shown up at the same time.

The corner of Fifth Avenue and East 50th Street, the block upon which "New" St. Patrick's Cathedral now stands, has belonged to the Archdiocese of New York since the early 1830s. A Jesuit school, a Catholic orphanage, and then the rectory of the Church of St. John the Evangelist have all occupied this site—a location considered so far north that New Yorkers referred to it as "out of town."

In 1853, Archbishop John Hughes surprised his congregation and all New Yorkers when he announced that he planned to erect a new cathedral uptown. And he had an architect in mind—James Renwick, the most respected architect in nineteenth-century America. Renwick had mastered a variety of architectural styles, but he was at his best when he was designing Gothic-style structures, and St. Patrick's would be his masterpiece. Yes, the exterior is lovely and impressive, but step inside.

Stand with your back to great bronze doors of the main entrance and you'll get the full effect of Renwick's design: elegant columns support the soaring ceiling vaults; a long main aisle sweeps up to the altar, which stands beneath a gilded baldacchino; and, visible beyond the altar, the heavenly deep blue of the stained-glass windows in the Lady Chapel.

Along the aisles are a series of chapels and side altars, many of them commemorating the various immigrant groups who came to New York. Each is beautiful, but one in particular stands out: the altar of St. Michael and St. Louis. It was designed by Tiffany & Company and was a gift of the Bouvier family, the ancestors of former First Lady Jacqueline Onassis.

Then there are two shrines that seem to be out of place in the cathedral—the much more modern shrines of St. John Neumann and of St. Elizabeth Ann Seton. That said, there are so many other beautiful things to see in St. Patrick's that you will be left spiritually uplifted.

St. Patrick's is open daily from 6:30 AM to 8:45 PM.

ASHEVILLE | Basilica of St. Lawrence
97 Hayward St. • Asheville, NC 28801
828-252-6042 • www.saintlawrencebasilica.org

For some 1,700 years, St. Lawrence has been one of the most venerated saints on the Catholic calendar. The Romans—he was martyred in Rome in 258—are especially attached to him.

He was a deacon who served Pope St. Sixtus I. After saying Mass in one of the catacombs, Sixtus and his clergy were surprised by a detachment of Roman soldiers who arrested them and took them away for martyrdom. Lawrence died an especially gruesome death—he was roasted on a grill. According to a story about his martyrdom, his last words were spoken to his executioner: "Turn me over," Lawrence said, "I'm done on this side." For this reason, St. Lawrence is the patron of cooks.

Construction of St. Lawrence Church was begun in 1904. Its architect was one of the greatest of his age, Rafael Guastavino, an immigrant from Barcelona, Spain, and a contemporary of the visionary and adventurous Barcelona architect, Antonio Gaudi. By great good luck, when the Catholics of Asheville were ready to build a substantial church, Guastavino was working in the neighborhood, constructing George Vanderbilt's palatial French chateau, Biltmore.

For the church, Guastavino drew his inspiration from the Romanesque churches of his home province, Catalonia, and one of his favorite building techniques, wide rounded arches to support the roof and the grand dome. He was especially pleased with the results, and asked to be buried in the basilica's crypt.

The works of art in the church were drawn from Europe and the United States. The altar was carved from a block of marble quarried in Tennessee. The statues of the saints were carved in Italy. Most of the stained-glass windows were fashioned in Munich, Germany.

Atop Our Lady's altar is a white marble sculpture of the Assumption of Mary. At the base of the altar are carvings of virgin saints, including St. Agnes, St. Catherine of Alexandria, Sr. Cecilia, and St. Rose of Lima—the first person born in the Americas to be canonized. The Blessed Sacrament altar, formerly the altar of St. Joseph, is a chapel for private adoration of Our Lord in the Eucharist.

For the hours of daily Masses, the times for confession, adoration of the Blessed Sacrament, and devotions, consult the parish website. You'll also find a calendar of regularly scheduled events that promote learning more about the faith, meeting and socializing with fellow parishioners, and participating in community outreach programs.

CHARLOTTE | St. Ann Church
3635 Park Rd. • Charlotte, NC 28209
704-523-4641 • www.stanncharlotte.org

We tend to think that great Catholic art is something from centuries ago. But the incredible five-panel mural that fills the sanctuary of the Church of St. Ann tells the parish and the world that great Catholic art is still alive, and one exceptional example has found a home here.

The mural is inspired by Jan van Eyck's 1432 masterpiece, *The Adoration of the Lamb*, displayed in the Cathedral of St. Bavo in Ghent, Belgium. The artist who painted St. Ann's mural is Andrew Hattermann of Illinois. In the central panel, God the Father is enthroned, and the Holy Spirit hovers over the scene. Below is the Lamb of God, standing upon an altar, surrounded by angels bearing the instruments of the Passion. Hattermann, like van Eyck, has filled the four adjacent panels with a host of saints.

The mural is the best example of fine art at St. Ann's, a church that is enriched by luminous stained-glass windows, a dozen life-size statues of saints, and a beautifully carved, eight-foot-high wooden pulpit dating from 1643 that was rescued from a closed Anglican church in England.

For most of American history, Catholics have been a religious minority in the South (Louisiana being an obvious exception). But in recent years, as the economy of the South has boomed, there has been a large southward migration of northerners, many of whom are Catholic. Southern bishops have been busy opening new parishes and schools; Southern pastors have been busy enrolling new parishioners. St. Ann's is one of those parishes that has been blessed by this influx of new people.

The pastor and his staff pride themselves on their beautiful liturgies, glorious music (St. Ann's has an excellent choir), and its community outreach. Parishioners visit the sick, the elderly, and the house-bound; twice a month, the parish collects nonperishable food for a local food pantry; and the parish contributes to the support of homeless women and children.

St. Ann's is a remarkable parish. Come for the great art, stay for the Mass, and meet the welcoming priests and parishioners who have made St. Ann's the destination church that it is.

For a schedule of Masses, confessions, devotions, and a calendar of special events, consult the parish website.

Fargo | Cathedral of St. Mary
604 Broadway • Fargo, ND 58102
701-235-4289 • www.cathedralofstmary.com

A disastrous fire delayed the opening of the Cathedral of St. Mary. It wasn't the church that burned—aside from its basement, St. Mary's didn't exist yet. The conflagration of 1893 swept through downtown Fargo, reducing many businesses and homes to heaps of blackened, smoldering timber.

Bishop John Shanley had set aside a large sum of cash to build his cathedral. But as his conscience wouldn't permit him to erect a fine church in the heart of a devastated city, he donated most of his building fund to rebuild downtown Fargo. Six years would pass before Bishop Shanley could afford to complete the construction of St. Mary's. By that time, thanks in part to the bishop's generosity, downtown Fargo had come back to life.

It is the two towers that give the cathedral its distinctive look: one is much shorter and smaller than the other, yet somehow this off-beat design works. Set in a niche of the smaller tower is a sculpture of the Blessed Mother, while statues of St. Peter and St. Paul flank the great window over the main entrances to the cathedral.

The interior of the cathedral is elegant, painted in shades of cream, pale blue, and trimmed with gold. Around the sanctuary arch are roundels with portraits of various saints, and above the tabernacle is a mural of Our Lady in Heaven, adored by angels. The shrines on either side of the main altar display lovely paintings of the Virgin and Child and Jesus as the Divine Mercy, a devotion that was especially dear to Pope St. John Paul II. The dark, beautifully carved woodwork of the bishop's throne, the pulpit, and the frames around the paintings of the shrines is especially fine.

Consult the cathedral website for times of Masses, confessions, Adoration of the Blessed Sacrament, and special events sponsored by the parish.

OHIO

CAREY | Basilica and National Shrine of
Our Lady of Consolation
315 Clay St. • Carey, OH 43316
419-396-7107 • www.olcshrine.com

Carey is a small town of about 1,600 households in northern Ohio. It's unusual for such a small community to have a shrine church that the Holy Father has designated a minor basilica, but that is what happened.

The National Shrine of Our Lady of Consolation was founded by a priest from Luxembourg, where Mary under this title is the patroness of the country. Carey had a large population of immigrants from Luxembourg, and some of the descendants of those nineteenth-century settlers still live in or around the town.

The statue venerated in the shrine is a replica of the original brought over from Luxembourg in 1875. The sculpture depicts the Blessed Virgin with the Christ Child in her arms, both of them dressed in elaborate robes.

The original white wooden shrine church from the 1870s still stands and is still used for early morning Mass and special events. Nearby is the far grander red-brick Romanesque-style basilica where the statue is enshrined today. Over the altar is a fine mural of Christ in majesty, seated upon a throne in heaven and attended by a host of saints and angels.

The basilica welcomes individual pilgrims as well as large pilgrim groups virtually year-round, but the event that draws the largest crowds is the solemn Mass and procession on the Feast of the Assumption, when the statue of Our Lady of Consolation is carried from the shrine church to the Shrine Park. A throng of visitors fills the campground and vacant parking lots for miles around. Since devotion to Our Lady of Consolation has grown among Eastern-Rite Catholics, the Conventual Franciscans who staff the shrine have added to their schedule of celebrations of the Eucharist during the pilgrimage the Divine Liturgy according to the ancient Chaldean and Syro-Malabar rites.

The landmark of the Shrine Park, and of the neighborhood, is an outdoor altar covered by a soaring baldachino, or canopy, crowned by a dome. Standing atop the dome is a tall, gilded statue of the Virgin and Child.

The basilica is open year-round, but the schedule of Masses does change by season. Consult the shrine's website for details. The Conventual Franciscans operate retreats; please call for availability.

CINCINNATI | Old St. Mary's Church
123 E. 13th St. • Cincinnati, OH 45202
513-721-2988 • www.oldstmarys.org

German-speaking Catholic immigrants built St. Mary's in a Cincinnati neighborhood that is still known as Over-the-Rhine. Opened in 1842, it is the oldest surviving Catholic church in the city.

The exterior is in the elegant Greek Revival style, while the interior is a bit baroque, a bit Romanesque. The church may display an eclectic approach to architecture, but it has a few consistent themes that has made Old St. Mary's a landmark in the Catholic landscape of Cincinnati: devotion to fine art, to fine music, and to solemn Masses—in English, German, and Latin—that reflect the Church's rich liturgical traditions.

One of the features that is peculiar to the church are the paintings over the altar of the Immaculate Conception, Our Lady as Queen of Heaven, and the Annunciation. Each is beautiful, though they are hung in rotation, so frequent visitors to the church can never be sure which painting they'll see on any given day.

Beneath the altar are the remains of an early Christian martyr, St. Martura.

The nineteenth century saw the systematic search for and rediscovery of forgotten catacombs in Rome. In the labyrinth of corridors and tunnels, archaeologists discovered the intact tombs of long-forgotten martyrs. Carefully and reverently, the relics were transferred to Church authorities in Rome, who then presented them to churches throughout the Catholic world.

In most cases, we know nothing for certain of these ancient saints other than their name and the fact of their martyrdom. St. Martura is one of those forgotten-but-still-venerated martyrs.

Consult the parish website for the schedule of daily Masses, when confessions are heard, days and times of Adoration of the Blessed Sacrament, and special events throughout the year.

NORTH JACKSON | Basilica and National Shrine of Our Lady of Lebanon

2759 N. Lipkey Rd. • North Jackson, OH 44451

330-538-3351 • www.ourladyoflebanonshrine.com

The overwhelming majority of Catholics in the United States belong to the Latin Rite. But there are other rites in full communion with the Holy Father, and who are as Catholic as any Irish or Italian monsignor.

The congregations of Maronite Catholics in the United States, who built and operate the Basilica of Our Lady of Lebanon, are united with Maronite Catholic congregations in Israel, Jordan, Syria, and Lebanon. Latin Rite Catholics can be confused about this, especially when they encounter a Catholic priest of one of the Eastern Churches who has a wife, or visit an Eastern Rite church and see a Divine Liturgy that is different from the Mass that they have known all their lives. Nonetheless, it would be worth your effort to spend some time exploring the rich mystical and liturgical traditions of the Eastern Churches.

The Maronites are proud that they alone of all the Eastern Churches have always been in union with Rome. Their community goes back to the era of the twelve apostles. The first Maronite Christians spoke Aramaic, the language of Jesus, Mary, Joseph, the apostles, and the first disciples of Our Lord.

In the early 1960s, as a sign that, as Americans, they had arrived, the Maronites from Lebanon who were living in Ohio and western Pennsylvania rallied to build a shrine in Mary's honor under her title, Our Lady of Lebanon. Standing in front of the shrine church is a stone tower around which is a spiral staircase that leads up to the top, where there is set a statue of the Blessed Mother, a replica of the one at the summit of a hill overlooking the Christian village of Harissa in Lebanon. Parishioners still speak of the day when the statue of Mary was installed on the tower. As the work crew wrestled the statue into place, a rainbow appeared in the sky, arching over Our Lady.

The shrine welcomes pilgrimage groups, but organizers of the pilgrimages are required to file a request, online, with the shrine's rector. If you will be passing through the area around August 15, the feast of the Assumption, plan to spend some time at the shrine, where every year there is a full day of liturgies, music, and other events to honor the Holy Mother of God.

OKLAHOMA

HULBERT | Our Lady of Clear Creek Abbey
5804 West Monastery Rd. • Hulbert, OK 74441
918-772-2454 • www.clearcreekmonks.org

This community of Benedictine monks is known as Clear Creek Abbey, so named for a stream that flows through the abbey grounds.

The community was founded in 1999 by a handful of monks, most of them Americans, from the abbey of Notre-Dame de Fontgombault in France. The monks belong the Solesmes Congregation of Benedictines, who back in the nineteenth century revived classic Gregorian chant and restored it to the Benedictine liturgy—a gift that has kept on giving for close to two hundred years now.

Visitors should know right from the start that the monks of Clear Creek celebrate the Mass and the Divine Office according to the Extraordinary Form, also known as the traditional (or Tridentine) Latin Rite. The monks are in complete union with Rome, so visitors and retreatants should not be concerned that they have wandered into some nest of wild-eyed schismatics.

The abbey at Clear Creek is still under construction, but since its founding, the monks have made excellent progress, with the monks' residence essentially complete and a significant part of the abbey church suitable for worship. Considering that when the monks arrived here from France they made their home in a stable, the current situation is an enormous leap forward.

The monks' architect, Professor Thomas Gordon Smith, renowned in Catholic circles for his splendid, somewhat updated designs that preserve the classic "look" of Catholic churches and religious houses, has designed a splendid monastic compounded for the Benedictines that will make this abbey a destination for Catholics in America for generations to come.

The monks welcome day-visitors as well as retreatants who wish to spend a few days participating in Clear Creek's life of prayer. Space is limited, so contact the abbey to make a reservation. Men are housed in a few rooms in the monastery. Women and families are housed in a guesthouse on the abbey grounds. Weekends and holy days tend to attract throngs of visitors to the abbey; guests who cannot be accommodated at the abbey are encouraged to stay at one of several nearby motels.

One of the high points of visiting Clear Creek is rising early and getting to the abbey church by 6:35 AM, when the priests file in to say their daily Mass at the many little side altars placed along the walls of the church. This was the custom in large religious communities for centuries, but, in general, not seen in this country for decades. To be in the chapel at or shortly after dawn as many Masses are being offered simultaneously is an unforgettable experience.

OREGON

**PORTLAND | National Sanctuary of Our Sorrowful Mother,
The Grotto**
8840 NE Skidmore St. • Portland, OR 97220
503-254-7371 • www.thegrotto.org

Most of the shrines mentioned in this book have well-tended, perhaps even landscaped grounds, but the National Sanctuary of Our Sorrowful Mother is a standout that combines the sanctity of churches, chapels, little shrines, and statuary with the glories of a renowned botanical garden. And because the sanctuary is set in the Pacific Northwest, where the climate tends to be mild, something is blooming every month of the year (consult the website's "What's in Bloom" schedule).

To make a pilgrimage to this sanctuary is to immerse yourself in the beauty of God's creation. The heart of the shrine is the grotto, carved into a cliff face of dramatic basalt rock. Above the altar is a to-scale, white marble replica of Michelangelo's Pieta.

From this outdoor chapel, begin your exploration of the grounds. Look for flowering Japanese magnolia and rhododendron in a riot of hues and colors in spring, Asia roses and daylilies in summer, mountain ash bearing flame-colored berries in autumn, camellias in winter, and giant California redwoods year-round—to name a tiny handful of the trees and flowering plants of the garden.

The interior of the stone-built Chapel of Mary is enriched with statues, mosaics, stained glass, and wonderful paintings, including a painting of the Coronation of the Blessed Virgin over the altar and murals of scenes from the life of the Holy Family along the side walls.

Amid the gardens are shrines of favorite saints of various ethnic groups, including Filipino, Vietnamese, Poles, and Lithuanians. St. Anne's Chapel, which has the look of a classic red one-room schoolhouse, was built as a chapel of the Blessed Sacrament during the first International Marian Congress, which was held here in 1934. There is also a replica of the labyrinth found on the floor of the Chartres Cathedral in France. In recent years, many visitors have found walking the labyrinth an effective way to deepen their practice of meditation.

The sanctuary is staffed by the Servite Fathers, who offer Mass daily, welcome pilgrimages, and with the generous assistance of volunteers, organize special events, such as the Grotto Concert Series and the Festival of Lights at Christmastime. Consult the website for a detailed schedule.

Laymen and laywomen are welcome to join group retreats held throughout the year, and clergy, religious, and seminarians are welcome to make private retreats at the sanctuary. Spiritual direction is available. For details, availability, and suggested donation, check the website or call the sanctuary.

SAINT BENEDICT | Mount Angel Abbey
1 Abbey Dr. • St. Benedict, OR 97373
503-845-3030 • www.mountangelabbey.org

Reviewers for online websites usually mention that Mount Angel Abbey is built in the Romanesque style—and it is! But so are lots of other abbeys, convents, and churches across America.

One building that sets Mount Angel apart is its library, which was not built in the Romanesque style: it was designed by one of the greatest architects of the twentieth century, Alvar Aalto of Finland. Considering that the jewel in the crown of the abbey library is its collection of rare medieval manuscripts—the earliest dating back to the twelfth century—one would expect a library that has a distinctly medieval look.

But Fr. Barnabas Reasoner, OSB, director of the library, was a man of sophisticated tastes; he took a chance and contacted Aalto, asking him if building a new library would interest him. Aalto signed on to the project and discounted his fee for the sake of the monks. The library showcases Aalto's love of gentle curves and buildings flooded with natural light. He also designed the furniture for the new library. It is a remarkable achievement, and very rare that a masterwork of modern architecture should find its way onto the grounds of a Catholic abbey.

Mount Angel was founded in the late nineteenth century by four German-speaking Benedictine monks from Switzerland. They settled near a community of German Catholics in a town then called Fillmore (now Mount Angel). The residents were so pleased by the arrival of German clergy that in their enthusiasm they pledged $1,200 to help build the abbey. Somebody threw in a cow.

The abbey possesses a small but very good collection of fine art—paintings, sculpture, and mosaics—including a lovely statue of the Virgin and Child dating from the 1500s. And some of the monks also paint (the technical term is "write") icons in the ancient Byzantine style.

Mount Angel is host to special events every summer—the Feast of St. Benedict, on or near the saint's feast day on July 11, and the Abbey Bach Festival. Call or consult the website for dates, times, and other details.

Over the years, Mount Angel has become a seminary that draws its aspirants for the priesthood from throughout the Pacific Northwest. Today, the seminarians are a lively mix of Anglos, Latinos, Vietnamese, and Filipinos.

You are welcome to make a retreat at Mount Angel. Choose from a daylong retreat to revive your spiritual life, make a private retreat, or join a group retreat. For availability and other information, contact the abbey.

PENNSYLVANIA

DOYLESTOWN | National Shrine of Our Lady of Czestochowa
654 Ferry Rd. • Doylestown, PA 18901
215-345-0600 • www.czestochowa.us

You'll sense it the moment you arrive. The National Shrine of Our Lady of Czestochowa is a holy place. It is intensely devoted to the Catholic faith, especially to Our Lady of Czestochowa, popularly known as the Black Madonna, as well as to fostering Polish culture and traditions and celebrating the achievements of Poles in the Old Country and here in America.

The Polish Pauline Fathers, who staff the shrine, are dedicated to their task of serving newly arrived Polish immigrants and Americans of Polish descent, offering a packed calendar of special events ranging from processions and novenas, to a Polish-American festival, to the blessing of motorcycles, and to retreats for recovering alcoholics.

During your visit, you may hear Polish spoken as much as English. And a glance at the shrine website reveals both English and Polish pages.

The Pauline Fathers have been here since 1953, about an hour by car north of Philadelphia. The first shrine chapel of the Black Madonna was in a converted barn, but by 1966, the current impressive shrine church and monastery were ready to be dedicated. Cardinal John Krol of Philadelphia—himself a son of Polish immigrants—dedicated the church and blessed the monastery, with President Lyndon Johnson among attending guests.

Over the main altar of the shrine church is a majestic bronze sculpture of the Blessed Trinity presenting a replica of the original icon of the Black Madonna to the faithful, as angels play trumpets to celebrate the glories of Mary under this title. Around the church are other shrines dedicated to saints beloved by Poles, such as St. Anne, and the patron of the Pauline Fathers, St. Paul the Hermit.

The Paulines offer Mass in Polish and English, confessions are heard daily, and there is a twice-weekly perpetual novena to Our Lady of Czestochowa, a monthly night vigil, and a youth group for young Catholics ages twelve to eighteen.

The shrine welcomes pilgrimages, but there are no accommodations on the grounds of the shrine. If you are planning to bring a group or attend one of the year-round retreats at the Ave Maria Retreat Center, contact the shrine.

Gettysburg | Fr. William Corby Monument
Gettysburg National Military Park
Hancock Avenue (near the George Weickert Farm)
Gettysburg, PA 17325 • 717-334-1124, extension 8023
www.gettysburg.stonesentinels.com/monuments-to-individuals/
father-william-corby

There are a lot of monuments and memorials on the Gettysburg battlefield, but this one is unique. It is a life-size bronze sculpture of a man with a long beard, his eyes raised to heaven, his left hand over his heart, and his right hand raised. Around his shoulders hangs a stole.

The man depicted is Fr. William Corby, a priest of the Congregation of the Holy Cross and a member of the faculty at Notre Dame in Indiana. He left the college to serve as a one of the chaplains to the renowned Irish Brigade. The sculpture depicts one of the most dramatic and memorable events in Fr. Corby's military career.

It was almost noon, July 2, 1863, and the 530 men of the Irish Brigade were resting on the eastern slope of Cemetery Ridge above the small town of Gettysburg when the order came for them to prepare to go into battle. As the men assembled, Fr. Corby climbed on top of a large rock and called for the men's attention. As they were about to go into battle, there was no time for him to hear the confession of every man of the brigade individually, he explained, but in such an emergency, the Catholic Church permitted a priest to grant general absolution.

He instructed them to recall their sins, beg God's pardon, and recite silently the Act of Contrition, just as they would if they were in a confessional. Then, Fr. Corby drew from a pocket of his black frock coat a violet stole. As he draped it around his neck, the men of the Irish Brigade—Catholics and non-Catholics alike—removed their caps and knelt on the grass.

Raising his right hand, he made the sign of the cross over the brigade as he recited the words of absolution: "May our Lord Jesus Christ absolve you, and I, by His authority, absolve you from every bond of excommunication and interdict, insofar as it lies within my power and you require; therefore, I absolve you from your sins, in the Name of the Father, and of the Son, and of the Holy Ghost. Amen."

While granting general absolution to soldiers who were about to go into battle was common in the Catholic countries of Europe, this was the first time it had ever occurred in the United States. When Fr. Corby had finished, the men rose from their knees and marched down the slope of Cemetery Ridge toward farmer John Rose's wheat field. The Irish would lose about two hundred men that afternoon.

PHILADELPHIA | Old St. Joseph's Church
321 Willings Alley • Philadelphia, PA 19106
215-923-1733 • www.oldstjoseph.org

Many of the thirteen original colonies had been founded as refuges for religious dissidents. Puritans found a safe haven in the New England colonies. Rhode Island welcomed all Christians—except Catholics. New Amsterdam—later New York—also welcomed all Protestants as well as Jews, but Catholics were not welcome. Maryland had been founded in 1634 as a sanctuary for Catholics, but a Protestant coup d'état a few decades later outlawed the public practice of the Catholic faith in the colony. Only Pennsylvania granted complete freedom of religion—or no religion at all—to its citizens. As a result, Catholics flocked to Pennsylvania.

In 1733, in Philadelphia, Jesuit priests established St. Joseph Church, at the time the only legitimate Catholic church in what would become the United States.

The parish website records how the next year, a complaint was filed with Pennsylvania's Provincial Council that, contrary to the laws of England, Mass was being celebrated at "the Romish

Chapell." The complainants called upon the colony's government to shut down St. Joseph's and prohibit the free exercise of the Catholic faith. The council consulted the Charter of Privileges granted to Pennsylvania by its founder, William Penn (a Quaker who had suffered for his faith in England), and found that religious freedom extended to all denominations, Catholics included. And so it is not going too far to say that Old St. Joseph's played an important part in the establishment of religious liberty in America.

Old St. Joseph's is hidden away in Willings Alley, east of Independence Hall. An attractive archway leads into a courtyard that opens onto the church. The exterior of St. Joseph's is plain red brick, but the interior is lovely—designed in an elegant Federal style.

Over the altar is an antique painting of the crucifixion, and on the ceiling is a painting of St. Joseph in glory. Daily and Sunday Masses tend to be crowded. But in off hours, the church is quiet, a perfect spiritual retreat from the noise of the city and the distractions of day-to-day life. It is a privilege to kneel and pray in a place that for nearly three hundred years has been so closely associated with the establishment of the Catholic faith in America.

PHILADELPHIA | Old St. Mary's Church
252 S. 4th St. • Philadelphia, PA 19106
215-923-7930 • www.oldstmary.com

A very short walk from Old St. Joseph's is Old St. Mary's, a parish established in 1763. From 1810 until 1838, the church was the cathedral of the Diocese of Philadelphia.

Like St. Joseph's, St. Mary's exterior is modest red brick. The interior was richly decorated. But a renovation in 1979 stripped away most of the church's artistic legacy, leaving it stark for worshippers today.

Nonetheless, historic furnishings from the old church have survived, including the baptismal font made in 1791, chandeliers from Independence Hall, and the throne of Bishop Henry Conwell, made in 1820. There is also a lovely marble sculpture of the Blessed Mother that some visitors to Old St. Mary's may find more appealing than the church itself.

During the American Revolution, members of Congress came to St. Mary's for ceremonies that celebrated the adoption of the Declaration of Independence and General George Washington's victory over the British at the Battle of Yorktown. John Adams attended Sunday vespers at St. Mary's and afterward as noted on the parish website, wrote a letter to his wife, Abigail, in which he said, "Here is everything that can lay hold of eye, ear, and imagination.... I wonder how Luther ever broke the spell."

PITTSBURGH | St. Anthony's Chapel
1704 Harpster St. • Pittsburgh, PA 15212
412-231-2994 • www.saintanthonyschapel.org

Over the main arch of the chapel is a Latin inscription that in English reads, "Here Lie the Saints in Peace." The inscription could not be more appropriate, since the chapel enshrines thousands of sacred relics of countless saints. It is likely that St. Anthony's has the largest relic collection in the United States.

The collection and the chapel were the lifelong work of Fr. Suitbert Mollinger, a Belgian immigrant and the heir to a substantial fortune. To build a chapel for his collection, he spent at least $300,000 of his own money and commissioned from artists in Europe the stained-glass windows and near life-size Stations of the Cross.

Visitors to the chapel may feel a bit overwhelmed—at last count, there were more than five thousand relics on display, many of them in superbly handcrafted reliquaries (the containers to protect and display sacred relics). Start in the chapel in the left transept of St. Anthony's—it displays a large cross that holds a splinter of the True Cross, a thorn from the Crown of Thorns, and a bit of stone from the Holy Sepulchre in Jerusalem. On St. Anthony's altar is a relic of the saint who is patron of this chapel.

Beneath the altar of the Blessed Sacrament are the complete skeletal remains of the martyr St. Demetrius. Beneath other altars are the skulls of other martyrs, including St. Stephana, St. Macharius, and some of the companions of St. Ursula.

The experience of taking in so many splendid works of art and such a vast array of relics can be overwhelming. To get a better sense of direction, join one of the regularly scheduled tours of the chapel. Typically, St. Anthony's is only open from 1 PM to 4 PM, so plan your visit accordingly. Contact the chapel website and the staff for general information and to schedule a tour.

St. Anthony's Chapel is a remarkable place, one of the most memorable shrines in Catholic America.

HARRISVILLE | Shrine of the Little Flower
35 Dion Dr. • Harrisville, RI 02830
401-568-8280 • www.sainttheresashrine.com

In 1923 Thérèse of Lisieux, popularly known as the Little Flower, had just been declared "blessed" in Rome by Pope Pius XI. Her beatification coincided with the founding of a new parish in Rhode Island, and the bishop urged the parishioners of the new church to dedicate it to Blessed Thérèse. In 1925 the parish celebrated the canonization—also by Pius XI—of their patron, and the church was renamed for St. Thérèse.

In the decades that followed, priests of the parish erected shrines around the parish church. These include: an outdoor Stations of the Cross, hand-carved by a sculptor from Quincy, Massachusetts, and a replica of the Holy Stairs. The original stairs, which are in Rome across the street from the Basilica of St. John Lateran, are said to be the stairs from the palace of Pontius Pilate, which Jesus climbed on the morning of Good Friday to hear Pilate condemn him to death.

In the 1970s, the shrine went into decline. The grounds became overgrown, and the sacred statuary around the church suffered from little maintenance and even from attacks by vandals. In the 1990s, a new pastor restored the shrine, and since then, new shrines and chapels have been added, including a chapel dedicated to the Seven Sorrows of Our Lady, a copy of Christ's tomb, a fifteen-decade living rosary, and brightly colored statues of Our Lady of Guadalupe.

The parish celebrates St. Thérèse in a solemn festival in the summer and welcomes groups of pilgrims throughout the year. Contact the parish to make arrangements for your group.

NEWPORT | St. Mary's Church
12 William St. • Newport, RI 02840
401-847-0475 • www.stmarynewport.org

St. Mary's has had a long, significant history. It was founded in 1828, making it the oldest Catholic parish in Rhode Island. While its formal name is Most Holy Name of Mary, Our Lady of the Isle, as is common throughout the United States, parishioners have referred to their church informally as St. Mary's—a name that has stuck.

The event that continues to draw visitors to this lovely Gothic church on Spring Street took place on September 12, 1953, when then-Senator John F. Kennedy married Jacqueline Bouvier. The pews were packed with wedding guests, and Archbishop (later Cardinal) Richard Cushing of Boston performed the ceremony and celebrated the Nuptial Mass. Over the next ten years, whenever the Kennedys visited Newport, they attended Mass at St. Mary's.

But the Kennedy-Bouvier wedding was not the only high-society wedding held at St. Mary's. The church's location in Newport, the summer playground of some of America's wealthiest families, has for years made it the church of choice for well-to-do, socially prominent Catholic couples. One especially memorable wedding took place in 1871, when a grandnephew of the emperor of France was married to a granddaughter of Daniel Webster.

The church was designed by Patrick Keely, one of Catholic America's most successful—not to mention prolific—architects. In his long career, he designed almost six hundred churches (including most cathedrals in New England) and hundreds of Catholic schools, convents, rectories, and other Catholic institutions.

The church is a Keely classic—he preferred the Gothic Revival architectural style which was so popular in the United States at the time. It is a beautiful church, and its chief treasures are the forty-two stained-glass windows, made in Austria in the late 1800s.

Consult the parish website for times of Masses and confessions, and for special events, such as organ concerts at the church. St. Mary's organ is one of the finest in New England.

Newport | Salve Regina University
100 Ochre Point Ave. • Newport, RI 02840
401-847-6650 • www.salve.edu

When you go to Newport, Rhode Island, you should eat oysters and visit the grand mansions along the oceanfront. The originals owners, without any trace of irony, called them "cottages."

Yet few visitors—Catholic or otherwise—know that several of these turn-of-the-twentieth-century mansions are to be found on the campus of Salve Regina University. In fact, the school opened when Ochre Court, a fifty-room French chateau, was donated to the Sisters of Mercy of Providence, who founded the college.

Over time, Salve Regina acquired seven estates that stood side by side along the Cliff Walk. To preserve the twenty-one historically and architecturally significant buildings on these estates, the university received a grant from the Getty Foundation.

The chapel, dedicated to Our Lady of Mercy, was consecrated in 2010. It is built of stone and shingle in a style that blends with the historic buildings on campus and in Newport's historic district. The interior of the chapel is plain, but the dark wooden pews and the dark wooden Tudor-style beams that support the ceiling warm up a sanctuary that otherwise would have been cold and uninviting. The chapel's greatest treasure, however, are stained-glass windows by John La Farge, one of the greatest American artists and designers of the late nineteenth century.

For a campus tour, contact the university.

PROVIDENCE | The Church of the Holy Name of Jesus
99 Camp St. • Providence, RI 02906
401-272-4515 • www.holynameprovidence.org

If you have been to Rome, you'll recognize the inspiration for the Church of the Holy Name of Jesus. The architect looked to one of the most ancient Roman basilicas, the basilica of St. Paul Outside the Walls, begun by Constantine, Rome's first Christian emperor, about the year 313.

The floor of the vestibule is covered with a fine mosaic—typical of early Roman churches. Inside the church, columns support the barrel vaults. Above the columns are sculptures of cherubs peeking out from acanthus leaves and busts of the twelve apostles.

Over the tabernacle is a semi-circular baldachino, or canopy, supported by columns of colored marble. The ceiling of the baldachino is covered with gold. Above the altar is a painting of Christ in majesty, attended by angels, and below him, saints seated on thrones as described in the New Testament Book of Revelation. The Blessed Mother's altar, dedicated to Our Lady of Lourdes, is especially lovely, and a replica of the famous Lourdes statue stands in a replica of the grotto.

Holy Name is a center for Catholics who love the old Latin Mass (known formally today as the Extraordinary form), with a Mass in this form every Sunday, as well as a special Mass for the parish's African American community.

The parish has several community outreach organizations, including a food pantry, a scholarship fund for the parish school, a group for Catholic young people, and another designed to make the men of the parish "strong men of God."

Consult the parish website or call the parish office for the hours of Mass and other information, including when the church is open.

SOUTH CAROLINA

CHARLESTON | St. Mary of the Annunciation Church
89 Hasell St. • Charleston, SC
843-329-3237 • www.saintmaryhasellst.org

Visitors to St. Mary's are enthusiastic about the beauty of the church's interior, the fine music, the liturgies and the excellent acoustics. In a town especially rich in historically and architecturally significant houses of worship—Charleston is often referred to as "the Holy City" of South Carolina—St. Mary's is a stand-out.

When the parish was established in 1789, it was the first and only Catholic church in the Carolinas and Georgia. Obviously Catholics who lived great distances from the church could not make the journey every Sunday for Mass, but the founding of St. Mary's inspired the foundation of other Catholic parishes in the Deep South.

Construction of the church you see today began in 1839. Built in the Greek Revival style, which was popular in America at the time, the simple exterior offers no hint of the loveliness of the church's interior.

It's the paintings that first attract the visitor's attention—there are almost thirty of them decorating St Mary's walls and ceiling. The oldest work of art in the church is the painting of the crucifixion over the main altar—it is the work of an American artist, John Cogdell, who donated it to the parish in 1814.

The stained glass windows were ordered from the Mayer Glassworks in Munich, Germany, a firm that supplied windows for countless Catholic churches and institutions in the nineteenth century. And in the choir loft is the church's organ, installed in 1874 to replace the church organ that had been destroyed by an artillery shell during the Union Navy's bombardment of Charleston toward the end of the Civil War.

On your way out of the church, walk through the old churchyard—the headstones trace the interesting history of St. Mary's and of the city of Charleston.

SOUTH DAKOTA

Yankton | House of Mary Shrine
142 Drees Dr. • Yankton, SD 57078
605-668-0121 • www.thehouseofmaryshrine.org

The chapel of the House of Mary Shrine was once a cabin that, through the inspiration of Ed and Jean English, was transformed into a sacred place in a remote corner of South Dakota.

Over the decades the site has expanded and has been extensively landscaped, largely by volunteers. Throughout the forty-five acres of the shrine are statues; small shrines; a meditation area; the Holy Innocents Garden, where visitors are urged to pray for the unborn; Stations of the Cross; two outdoor rosaries, one with beads of stone and the other with beads of wood; and a Way of the Saints area, comprised of low pillars with images of the favorite saints of the area's donors. There are also cabins available for those who would like to make a retreat.

If you are feeling up to it, climb the hill to see the three large wooden crosses that overlook Lewis and Clark Lake. The view is magnificent, and from this vantage point, it is not unusual to spot eagles soaring overhead.

During the summer months, Mass is said here once a week. Call or check the website for days and times Masses are celebrated, and for a schedule of events, which include an Easter sunrise service, a May crowning, and a rosary rally.

TENNESSEE

MEMPHIS | St. Jude Children's Research Hospital
262 Danny Thomas Pl. • Memphis, TN 38105
901-578-2042, 800-877-5833 • www.stjude.org

Danny Thomas was a struggling actor with a family when he knelt before a statue of St. Jude and asked the patron of impossible cases to help him. In return, Thomas promised to find a way to honor St. Jude publicly with a shrine. Thomas's prayer was answered, and the St. Jude Children's Research Hospital he founded is the fulfillment of a grateful man's promise.

St. Jude Hospital is internationally recognized as one of the foremost facilities for treating—and defeating—cancer and other serious diseases that afflict children. To relieve some of the pressure from families, St. Jude issues the families meal cards for the hospital cafeteria and gift cards for local grocery stores. It also offers free accommodations.

The hospital welcomes visitors ages sixteen and up, but visitors must call in advance to reserve space on a guided tour. If you prefer, you can take a self-guided tour of the Danny Thomas ALSAC Pavilion, a beautiful building in the Moorish style, which displays memorabilia from Thomas's impressive career, culminating with the Congressional Medal of Honor. The Pavilion also has a nondenominational chapel. There is another chapel on the first floor of the Patient Care Center.

The Danny and Rose Marie Thomas Memorial Garden is a lush oasis in the center of downtown Memphis, and the site of the burial crypt of Danny and Rose Marie.

NEW HOPE | Shrine of Our Lady Virgin of the Poor
Burns Island Rd. • New Hope, TN 37380
423-837-7068

Down a Tennessee back-country road in Marion County is a little stone chapel set amid 600 acres of fields and woods on what had once been a family farm.

The stone chapel with its steep roof and small cupola was built by Benedictine monks in 1982. It is a replica of a chapel in Banneux, Belgium, where Mary appeared in 1933 to a twelve-year-old girl, Mariette Beco. Our Lady described herself as "the Virgin of the Poor," and said that she had come "to relieve suffering." The chapel in Belgium stands on or near the spot where the Blessed Mother came to Mariette. After three investigations by Church authorities in Belgium, the apparitions were declared authentic by the bishop of Liege.

The Tennessee shrine has a large mosaic over the door of the apparition of Our Lady to Mariette. Inside the chapel is another mosaic of the crucifixion. On the altar is a statue of the Virgin of the Poor.

This is a private shrine, rather than one administered and staffed by the local diocese. Call for information regarding opening hours and if any Masses, devotions, or special events are scheduled at the shrine.

TEXAS

DICKINSON | Shrine of the True Cross
300 Fm 517 Rd. E • Dickinson, TX 77539
281-337-4112 • www.truecrosschurch.org

What is known today as the Shrine of the True Cross was originally the Church of St. Joseph, built to serve the large number of Italian immigrants, most of them from Sicily, who had settled in the area between Galveston and Houston.

In the 1930s, as fascism, communism, and secularism spread across the world, the parish priest at St. Joseph's, Fr. Thomas Carney, began to preach on the subject of devotion to the Holy Cross as a sure defense against the errors of his time.

Bishop Christopher Byrne of Galveston encouraged Fr. Carney's efforts to spread this devotion, and in 1936, he presented the parish with a relic of the True Cross which he had brought to Dickinson from Rome. Fr. Byrne received further support from Cardinal Pietro Fumasoni-Biondi, then the prefect of the Sacred Congregation for the Propagation of the Faith (now called the Congregation for the Evangelization of Peoples). He bestowed upon the parish the rare privilege of associating it with Rome's Basilica of the Holy Cross, built on the site of the palace of St. Helena, who discovered the True Cross in 326. The relic is still enshrined in the basilica.

The relic consists of two tiny splinters of the True Cross set together to form a cross. It is mounted in a gilded cross, surrounded by a gilded crown of thorns. You will find it behind a glass panel in a large cross-shaped stone shrine.

The design of the church is contemporary, but most of the artwork and furnishings are traditional.

For hours of Mass, confessions, and devotions, consult the shrine's website. To enter the Perpetual Adoration Chapel, stop by the parish office to receive the security code.

HILL COUNTRY | Painted Churches of the Texas Hill Country

There are fifteen painted churches in the Texas Hill Country, all of them built by Czech (known as Bohemians in the late nineteenth and early twentieth centuries) and German immigrants. They recreated in this land, so far from their homes, the type of church architecture and decoration they had known and loved in their native villages.

The twenty-five-county region of Central Texas and South Texas includes portions of the San Antonio and Austin metropolitan areas.

Once thriving parishes, most of the painted churches now have limited Mass schedules. Still, they are lovingly maintained, often by men and women who are parishioners.

Contact information, as you'll see, is erratic. Some churches do not have a website or do not list a phone number. But the Schulenburg Chamber of Commerce can help you. For more information, call or visit the Schulenburg Chamber of Commerce,

618 N. Main St., Schulenburg, TX, 979-743-4514. Call well in advance, and ask if they can arrange a guided tour of the churches you would like to visit.

A brief look at four of the fifteen churches follows:

LA GRANGE | *St. John the Baptist Church*

A mong the Painted Churches, St. John the Baptist is a bit low-key. There is a good deal of fine stenciling, and the main altar and old statues are lovely—especially the statue of St. John baptizing Jesus, which stands above the tabernacle. But there isn't the explosion of color that you'll find in most of the other painted churches. Nonetheless, there are many fine touches—the stained glass with inscriptions in Czech, and detailed veining on the woodwork to create a faux-marble look.

7850 Mensik Rd. • La Grange, TX 78945

DUBINA | *Saints Cyril and Methodius Church*

A t first glance, Saints Cyril and Methodius Church resembles any American country church, but the swooping steeple is straight out of Prague. The walls, the ceiling, the inside of the Gothic arches, and the arch over the sanctuary are all embellished with delightful stenciling in folk art patterns. The finely carved altars are of dark wood, brightened by painted statues.

FM Rd. 1383 • Dubina, TX 78956

979-725-8461

FLATONIA | *Assumption of the Blessed Virgin Mary*

Assumption of the Blessed Virgin Mary (parishioners know it as St. Mary's) is unusual for its blue wash on the ceiling and its paintings of ancient Christian symbols, such as the triangle, representing the Blessed Trinity, with the all-seeing eye of God in its center. The vaults are covered with landscape scenes, and along the walls, in addition to the Stations of the Cross, are framed paintings of saints and events from the Bible. In the sanctuary stands an elaborately carved pulpit, trimmed with gold, with a sounding board above, a feature found in Catholic and Protestant churches for centuries as a way to amplify the preacher's voice before there were microphones.

821 FM 1295 • Flatonia, TX 78941
361-596-4674 • www.stmaryspraha.org

SCHULENBURG | *Nativity of the Blessed Virgin Mary Church*

This is the queen of the painted churches. The Nativity of the Blessed Virgin Mary is a riot of color. It is hard to find a space that has not been painted. The wooden columns that support the arches have been given a faux finish to resemble priceless colored marble. Statues of the saints are everywhere, from the altars to pedestals mounted on the columns to the pulpit which is surrounded by seated saints. And over the main altar, instead of painting or a sculpture, there is a stained-glass window of the crucifixion.

2833 FM 2672 • Schulenburg, TX 78956
979-743-3117 • www.stmary-highhill.com

HOUSTON | Our Lady of La Vang Church
12320 Old Foltin Rd. • Houston, TX 77086
281-999-1672 • www.lavangchurch.org

The Blessed Virgin Mary under the title Our Lady of La Vang is the patroness of Vietnam and defender of all Vietnamese Catholics.

In 1798, during a period of fierce persecution of the Church, a band of Catholic villagers fled into the southeast Asian mountains of La Vang, hoping that the dense jungle would conceal them from the authorities.

The refugees faced terrible hardships—hunger, disease, even attacks by wild animals. Every night, the villagers gathered under an ancient banyan tree to pray the rosary. One night the Virgin Mary, holding the Christ Child in her arms, appeared to the villagers. She consoled them and gave them some practical advice—if they boiled the leaves of certain trees they would be healed of their ailments. Finally, she asked that a shrine be erected on the spot, promising that she would hear the prayers of all who appealed to her.

After the Vietnam War, when South Vietnam was overrun by Communist troops from North Vietnam, a great wave of refugees left the country, hoping to settle in other Asian nations, such as the Philippines, or to emigrate to far-off lands, such as the United States. According to W. Courtland Robinson in his book *Terms of Refuge: The Indochinese Exodus and the International Response*, it is estimated that, between 1975 and 1997, 1.6 million Vietnamese left their homeland.

Catholic bishops and laity in the Unites States have been generous in helping the refugees settle into their new home. Vietnamese Catholic parishes, many of them dedicated to Our Lady of La Vang, can be found throughout America. The parishes have become centers not only of the faith, but also of Vietnamese culture and language.

The Houston parish has a large shrine in front of the church. The statue of Our Lady and the Child Jesus stands in a stylized representation of the famous banyan tree. Inside the church is a smaller statue of Our Lady of La Vang, which is carried in procession through streets.

If you plan to attend Mass at the Church of Our Lady of La Vang, contact the church office for the Mass schedule and when bilingual Masses are celebrated.

San Antonio | Alamo
300 Alamo Plaza • San Antonio, TX 78205
210-225-1391 • www.thealamo.org
The Tomb of Fallen | Cathedral of San Fernando
115 Main Plaza • San Antonio, TX
210-227-1297 • http://www.sfcathedral.org/

Every American has heard of the Battle of the Alamo, the heroic-but-hopeless defense put up by a few dozen Texans against an army from Mexico that numbered in the thousands. It is a national historic site, not to mention a historic shrine revered by Texans.

But most visitors overlook the fact that before the defenders, through the sacrifice of the lives for the cause of liberty and independence, made the site holy ground in the political sense, it was already holy ground as a mission founded by a Franciscan priest to bring the local Native American tribes into the Catholic faith.

The Alamo's story begins in 1718, when Franciscan Father Antonio de San Buenaventura y Olivares blessed the site of a mission he named San Antonio de Valero. Six years later, he moved his mission to a more promising location, and this is where visitors find the Alamo today. It remained an outpost of Catholicism in Texas until 1792, when the Mexican government seized the property.

In the years since 1836, when Lieutenant Colonel William B. Travis and his men made their last stand at the Alamo, the mission has suffered a great deal of damage. The chapel survives and so does the priest's residence, known as the convent, but the rest of the mission compound has been lost. Nonetheless, when you visit the Alamo, step into the old, battered chapel and say a prayer for the missionary fathers and their converts, and pray for the souls of the brave men who died at the Alamo.

For many visitors, the appearance of the Alamo comes as a surprise, maybe even as a disappointment. In the movies that have been made about the Battle of the Alamo, the church looks grand, even monumental. In fact, it is very small. And, of course, it is no longer on the dusty outskirts of a sleepy colonial town, but in the noisy heart of downtown San Antonio, with a spacious parking lot across the street. Visitors who brace themselves for these realities about the shrine will probably enjoy their experience more than someone whose ideas about the Alamo are based on the 1960 John Wayne movie of the same name.

There is another site in San Antonio associated closely with the Alamo that most visitors miss. Enshrined in a white marble sarcophagus in the vestibule of the Cathedral of San Fernando lie the remains of the fallen defenders of the mission.

Since the Mexican government regarded the defenders of the Alamo as rebels, they were not given a decent burial. Instead, Santa Ana's troops piled up the corpses and burned them. After the Mexican army had moved on, Texans gathered up the remains, sealed them in a chest, and buried it in the sanctuary of San Fernando. In 1936, the chest was rediscovered and the remains moved to the vestibule.

SAN JUAN | Basilica of Our Lady of San Juan del Valle National Shrine
400 N. Virgen de San Juan Blvd. • San Juan, TX 78589
956-787-0033 • www.olsjbasilica.org

As is the case with so many devotions among Latinos in the United States, devotion to Our Lady of San Juan del Valle has its origins in Mexico, in the state of Jalisco. In 1623, a little girl took a nasty fall and died. Her family implored Our Lady to intercede for the child; miraculously, the little girl was restored to life.

Mexican Americans may have already been invoking Our Lady of San Juan when, in 1949, a parish priest in San Juan, Texas, asked a wood carver in Guadalajara to make a reproduction of the statue of Our Lady of San Juan del Valle. The priest placed it in his little church, but the shrine attracted such large crowds that the local bishop approved a plan for a much larger church.

Sixteen years later, in 1970, fifty priests gathered at the shrine to concelebrate Mass. Suddenly a small plane crashed into the roof of the shrine, and the resulting fireball engulfed the church in flames. Although the pilot lost his life in the crash, the priests and the congregation all escaped unharmed. Two priests and the sacristan risked their lived to rescue the Blessed Sacrament and the statue of Our Lady.

To replace the destroyed shrine, a new, even larger shrine church was erected in a distinctly modern style. The focal point of the church is the statue of Our Lady standing in a circular frame, golden rays radiating from her, with a crown upon her head and elaborately embroidered robes covering everything but her face.

Most of the Masses at this thriving Latino parish are in Spanish or are bilingual (with prayers, readings, and hymns in Spanish and English). Two Masses on Sunday are accompanied by a mariachi band.

In addition to the celebration of Mass and hearing of confessions, the shrine has a busy schedule of devotions—consult the shrine website for days and times.

According to the Texas State Historical Association, between ten to twenty thousand pilgrims come to pray at the Basilica of Our Lady of San Juan del Valle every week, with an annual total of about one million visiting the shrine. The demand for Masses to be offered for the faithful departed or other intentions is so strong that the priests have asked their parishioners to limit their requests for Masses to three per year, in order to accommodate the requests of pilgrims.

Regarding crowds, if possible, visit the basilica on a weekday.

UTAH

Salt Lake City | Cathedral of the Madeleine
331 East South Temple • Salt Lake City, UT 84111
801-328-8941 • www.utcotm.org

The first thing you'll notice once you step inside the Cathedral of the Madeleine are the astonishing paintings on the ceilings, on the walls, on the columns, even on the organ pipes. It is very much like stepping inside one of the churches in Italy where Renaissance masters labored to transform what had been a bare interior into one of the most beautiful things this side of heaven.

And consider that the location of the Catholic cathedral is in Salt Lake City, the Mormon church's Rome. It shouldn't surprise us if the extraordinarily beautiful Madeleine is saying to our brothers and sisters in the faith to say, "Yep, we're here, too!"

When the cathedral was consecrated in 1909, it was bare. Then in 1917, Salt Lake City received a new bishop, Joseph S. Glass, a man with a deep appreciation of fine art. To bring beauty to his cathedral, Bishop Glass hired John Theodore Comes, one of the most prominent architects and interior designers of his day, to create a new Cathedral of the Madeleine, filled with sacred imagery and color. It was Comes who designed the shrine of St. Mary Magdalene, the cathedral's patron saint, and the other shrines within the church. The result is the complex-but-harmonious creation you see today.

Some visitors may find the Stations of the Cross a bit jarring. In the first place, they are not the traditional fourteen Stations; they are a post-Vatican-II-inspired, Bible-based version. Consequently, you find no stations of Jesus meeting his sorrowful mother, or Veronica wiping the face of Jesus. Tradition aside, the paintings of the Stations are very interesting. They are the work of a Utah artist, Roger Wilson, and were installed in the early 1990s. The very bright colors are drawn from the traditional styles of Native American, Latino, and Anglo artists. Around each scene are ancient Christian symbols, as well as plants and animals of the Southwest that have significance in this part of the United States.

The Chapel of the Blessed Sacrament is covered with paintings of saints and angels, with a vault painted with a dazzling array of golden stars. The tabernacle is a soaring tower, inspired by the tabernacle towers that were so popular in German churches during the Middle Ages. For the space above the high altar, artist Felix Lieftucher painted the Trinity attended by a host of angels and saints.

There is so much to see that by just wandering about the cathedral you are likely to miss a great deal of what is beautiful and interesting. The Madeleine offers guided tours—contact the cathedral office for reservations.

For opening hours and the times of Mass, confessions, and benediction of the Blessed Sacrament, consult the cathedral website.

VERMONT

Isle La Motte | Shrine of St. Anne
92 St. Anne's Rd. • Isle La Motte, VT 05463
802-928-3362 • www.saintannesshrine.org

This a beautiful spot, set on the shores of majestic Lake Champlain, about ten miles south of the Canadian border.

In 1666 French troops came to Isle La Motte to erect a fort, one of a string of outposts built to defend French settlements in Canada from attacks by Native American tribes. Inside the fort, the soldiers erected a chapel that they dedicated to St. Anne, the mother of the Virgin Mary and the grandmother of Jesus Christ. It was here that the first Mass was said in Vermont, and here that Vermont received its first episcopal visit when St. Francois Laval, bishop of Quebec, traveled by canoe to Isle La Motte to confirm Native Americans who had converted to the Catholic faith.

The fort didn't last long. The government in Canada recalled the troops, and the outpost was abandoned. More than two hundred years later, a priest of the Diocese of Burlington raised funds to purchase the land on which the fort had stood and begin construction of a new chapel of St. Anne.

Today, the shrine comprises a charming little chapel crowned by an onion-shaped dome and a spacious outdoor pavilion where, typically in the late spring, summer, and early fall, to accommodate crowds of pilgrims, Mass is said. Placed around the grounds is an ever-growing collection of sculptures of Our Lady, St. Anne, and other saints, as well as a statue of Samuel de Champlain, who explored the lake and the islands in 1609. There are also outdoor Stations of the Cross that overlook the lake.

The chapel is small and intimate. Above the altar stands a fine statue of St. Anne with Mary as a young girl—the gift in the 1890s of Breton priests (St. Anne is especially venerated in the French province of Brittany).

The shrine welcomes retreatants. There are five cabins, each with a kitchen and bedrooms—with bunk beds—for up to sixteen people. There is also a large, beautifully designed building for meetings, meals, and socializing around a large stone fireplace.

The shrine is open from late May until early October. Contact the shrine office for exact dates. Mass is said here daily, and there are many special events and pilgrimages throughout the summer, culminating with the Feast of St. Anne on July 26.

JAMAICA | Our Lady of Ephesus House of Prayer
35 Fawn Ledge Lane • Jamaica, VT 05343
802-896-6000 • www.ourladyofephesushouseofprayer.org

There is an ancient tradition that, after the ascension of Christ, St. John the apostle and evangelist went with the Blessed Virgin Mary to Ephesus in what is now Turkey. At the time, Ephesus was the greatest city in the eastern portion of the Roman Empire.

In the nineteenth century, Blessed Anne Catherine Emmerich had a vision of a house in Ephesus that she said was the home of the Virgin Mary. In 1881, a French priest found the remains of a house that fit the description given by Blessed Anne Catherine.

The house was restored, and although the Catholic Church has never stated that the house is the actual dwelling place of Mary, three popes—Paul VI, St. John Paul II, and Benedict XVI—have all come to Ephesus to pray in the house. Interestingly, both Christians and Muslims come to pray here (the Koran reveres Jesus as a prophet, and also reveres Mary, his Mother).

Today, the remains of Ephesus is one of the world's most magnificent archaeological sites. On the edge of the site, on a hill overlooking the Aegean, is a small stone house that is said to have been the home of Our Lady.

Our Lady of Ephesus House of Prayer is a replica of the house in Ephesus built by the Tarinelli family. It is a lovely stone chapel that welcomes pilgrims. There are special events throughout the year, including, during Lent, following the outdoor Stations of the Cross, usually on snowshoes (this is Vermont after all).

It is possible to make a retreat here. Contact the House of Prayer for availability and for the suggested donation. From time to time, Mass is said in the chapel—call for more information.

VIRGINIA

Alexandria | St. Mary Church
310 S. Royal St. • Alexandria, VA 22314
703-836-4100 • www.stmaryoldtown.org

In the heart of Alexandria's historic Old Town stands St. Mary Church, the oldest Catholic church in Virginia. It was founded in 1795, just four years after the ratification of the US Bill of Rights, which guaranteed freedom of religion in the United States.

To take advantage of their newly acquired religious liberty, Catholics in Alexandria, Virginia, planned to build what they had never had—a Catholic church. A driving force behind the foundation of the parish was a veteran of the American Revolution, Colonel John Fitzgerald. There is a tradition in the parish that the first contribution to the St. Mary's building fund came from George Washington.

As is the case with most Catholic churches over the centuries, the appearance of St. Mary's has evolved. The most recent renovation restored the simple look of the original church, in keeping with the elegant-but-subdued style that was favored during the first years of America's independence. While you're here, wander through the church's cemetery to see the resting place of generations of parishioners, including five men who fought in the American Revolution.

Three special highlights of the church are the vibrant stained-glass windows, the beautiful white marble sculptures of Our Lady and St. Joseph, and the lovely paintings on the ceiling. Compared to much more elaborately decorated churches, such as St. John Cantius in Chicago, St. Mary is low-key, but take your time and you'll come to appreciate the beauty of the place.

St. Mary's is a busy parish. Consult the parish website for Mass times, and days and hours of adoration and benediction of the Blessed Sacrament, recitation of the rosary, and other devotions.

WASHINGTON

Olympia | Our Lady of Perpetual Help Shrine
St. George Byzantine Catholic Church
9730 Yelm Highway SE • Olympia, WA 98513
360-459-8373 • www.stgeorgeolympia.com

Byzantine Catholics and other Catholics of the Eastern Rite practice tremendous patience with many of their brothers and sisters of the Latin Rite who mistakenly believe that Eastern Rite Catholics are not really Catholic and even confuse them with Orthodox Christians.

One thing that Catholics of the Eastern and Western rites have in common is veneration of the icon of Our Lady of Perpetual Help. It was written, which is the preferred term in the East for the creation of icons, in the fifteenth century or a little earlier, probably by an artist on the island of Crete. It is said that, in 1499, an Italian merchant traveling through Crete saw the icon, stole it, and brought it back to his house in Rome. From the merchant's home, the icon was installed in several Roman churches until 1865, when Blessed Pope Pius IX entrusted the icon to the Redemptorists, who spread devotion to Our Lady under this title throughout the Western world. (She was already well-known and well-loved in the East).

To express their devotion to the Mother of God under this title, the clergy, parishioners, and friends of the Church of St. George erected on the church grounds a small, charming chapel in which to house their copy of the Perpetual Help icon. The shrine blends the rustic architecture of the Pacific Northwest with traditional Eastern elements, including gilded onion domes on the roof.

Every summer there is an annual pilgrimage to the shrine that combines the liturgy and devotions of the Byzantines with an all-American cookout.

To visit the shrine, which is about sixty-five miles south of Seattle, or to join the next Byzantine Catholic pilgrimage, consult the parish website.

WEST VIRGINIA

WHEELING | St. Joseph Retreat Center

137 Mount St. Joseph Rd. • Wheeling, WV 26003

304-232-8160 • www.stjosephretreatcenter.org

Spring and summer are the best seasons to visit the St. Joseph Retreat Center. The Sisters of St. Joseph of Wheeling are enthusiastic gardeners, and when the weather turns warm, the gardens of their motherhouse are overflowing with lush flowerbeds. Of course, fall isn't bad either, with the woods that surround the motherhouse ablaze with color.

The retreat center was originally a private home. The public areas on the first floor still have the original mantelpieces, the inlaid walnut floors, and paintings imported from Italy. It is not unusual for retreat houses to be furnished with castoffs, but St. Joseph's public areas have handsome, comfortable furnishings suitable to the style of the house. Outside are lovely shaded patios and other sitting areas where retreatants can meditate upon the beauty of God's creation.

The retreat center is a small place, with only seven private rooms and one apartment. There is a shared bath. Meals are served in the dining room of the Mount St. Joseph motherhouse. There is also a chapel where Mass is offered daily.

Located in the hills of West Virginia, St. Joseph Retreat Center is a quiet, serene place to withdraw from the noise and busyness of the world to renew and deepen your relationship with God. The center offers private retreats, group retreats, and individual directed retreats. Among other special events, throughout the year St. Joseph's hosts week-long retreats led by a guest speaker.

Rooms at the retreat center are $35 per night, $50 nightly for the apartment; meals are extra. Bed linens and towels are provided.

WISCONSIN

CHAMPION | Shrine of Our Lady of Good Help
4047 Chapel Dr. • Champion, WI 54229
920-866-2571 • www.shrineofourladyofgoodhelp.com

Over the years in the United States, there have been self-proclaimed seers or visionaries who claimed to have seen and/or received messages from Our Lord, Our Lady, or various saints. And that is what makes the Shrine of Our  Lady of Good Help unique—in the correct sense of the word—in America. The apparition of the Blessed Virgin Mary to a Belgian immigrant, Marie Adele Joseph Brise, is the only one in the United States to be decreed authentic by the Catholic Church. The statement of authenticity, published by Bishop David Ricken of Green Bay on the Feast of the Immaculate Conception, December 8, 2010, permits faithful Catholics to make pilgrimages to the shrine and perform acts of devotion there.

Adele Brise was twenty-eight years old when she was visited three times by the Blessed Mother, who introduced herself as "the Queen of Heaven, who prays for the conversion of sinners." She urged Adele to pray for sinners, too, and to gather the children of the settlers living in what Mary called "this wild country" and teach them the basics of the Catholic faith. Adele did her best to do as Our Lady asked and started a community of religious sisters to teach children their prayers, the catechism, and how to prepare to receive the grace of the sacraments.

Adele's father built a small oratory near the site of the apparitions, and in 1861, as word spread, the first group of pilgrims arrived at the tiny shrine. Ten years later, there was a school, a convent, and an enlarged chapel. When the devastating Peshitgo Fire swept through the region, the flames did not touch any of the structures on the site, or anything within a five-acre radius around them.

The shrine church you see today was consecrated in 1942. Over the main altar of the upper church is a lovely statue of the Virgin and Child. In the lower church are many crutches that were left behind by pilgrims who were healed through the intercession of Our Lady of Good Help. On the grounds are the Stations of the Cross and a Rosary Walk.

Now that the apparition of the Blessed Mother has been confirmed by the Church, the number of pilgrims to this remote spot has increased. Consult the shrine's website for upcoming events, as well times of daily Mass, confessions, and devotions, and to confirm the shrine's hours of operation (typically from 7 AM to 7 PM every day of the year).

In August 2016, the US Conference of Catholic Bishops raised the Shrine of Our Lady of Good Help to a National Shrine.

MILWAUKEE | St. Joan of Arc Chapel
Marquette University • 1250 W. Wisconsin Ave.
Milwaukee, WI 53233 • 414-288-6873
www.marquette.edu/st-joan-of-arc-chapel

On the campus of Marquette University stands a fifteenth-century chapel that has a connection to St. Joan of Arc. In 1926, Gertrude Hill Gavin, the heiress to a railroad fortune, saw the then-tumbled down-five-century-old chapel in the village of Chasse in the Rhone Valley in southeast France, and decided to buy it and relocate it to her estate on Long Island.

Seven years later, Pope Pius XI granted Gavin permission to have Mass said in the chapel, which she had renamed in honor of St. Joan of Arc (originally, the chapel had been dedicated to St. Martin of Tours).

Gavin furnished the chapel with a thirteenth-century altar and an artifact known as the Joan of Arc Stone. It is said that the stone comes from a church in France where Joan once prayed before battle; then, as an act of humility, she bent down and kissed the stone.

Tour guides point out the stone set in the wall behind the altar and encourage visitors to touch it and then the stones surrounding it—the St. Joan Stone is colder than its neighbors. (It's true. I visited the chapel years ago and found that the stone is indeed colder.)

In 1962, the Gavin estate passed to the Rojman family, who donated the chapel to Marquette University.

Mass is said in the chapel on weekdays during most of the school year. Call the Office of Campus Ministry to learn days and hours when the chapel is open to visitors and when Mass will be celebrated.

Peshtigo | Peshtigo Fire Museum
400 Oconto Ave. • Peshtigo, WI 54157
715-582-3244 • www.peshtigofiremuseum.com

Unless you hail from Wisconsin, it's unlikely that you've ever heard of the Peshtigo Fire. It was a forest fire, the worst ever seen in the United States. It was especially destructive in the rural town of Peshtigo. The conflagration reached Peshtigo on October 8, 1871, and ripped through the town. When the fire moved on, it left more than one thousand residents dead and had reduced every building in Peshtigo to ashes.

As terrible as the Peshtigo Fire was, it was displaced in the newspapers by an eerie coincidence—the same day that Peshtigo burned, the Chicago Fire swept across the city, driving thousands of residents (including Mary Todd Lincoln, widow of Abraham Lincoln) from their homes to safety along the shores of Lake Michigan.

A collection of artifacts from the Peshtigo Fire is displayed in a deconsecrated church that stands on the site of the town's Catholic parish, St. Mary's. As the fire raged, Fr. Peter Pernin took the tabernacle from the altar and ran to the Peshtigo River, where he submerged the sacred chest. As a result of Fr. Pernin's courage and foresight, the tabernacle survived intact, unlike the church and its furnishings, which were destroyed. The tabernacle is displayed in the museum, the only artifact undamaged by the conflagration.

Adjacent to the museum is a cemetery where many of the victims of the fire lie buried. Some bodies could be identified, but hundreds more were burned beyond recognition and rest in a Mass grave marked by a handsome monument.

Open May to October. Call ahead for days and hours of operation.

WYOMING

Lander | Wyoming Catholic College
306 Main St. • Lander, WY 82520
877-332-2930 • www.wyomingcatholiccollege.com

When was the last time you heard of a Catholic college that required all students to learn how to groom, train, and ride horses? Probably never.

But this is just one facet of what makes Wyoming Catholic College unique. The state of Wyoming is still sparsely populated. Outdoor sports not only serve as entertainment; in many situations, they provide essential skills. So the college operates seminars where all of its students acquire the skills to survive safely in the outdoors during summer and winter. Learning how ride and care for a horse is an extension of this program and is as natural in Wyoming as the quest for the best pizza is in New York City.

The college traces its origins to a talk given by Bishop David Ricken, then of Cheyenne (now of Green Bay, Wisconsin) to a group of lay leaders of his diocese. The bishop spoke of his passion for promoting Catholic education in Wyoming and pointed out that there was no Catholic college in the state. At that conference, the idea for Wyoming Catholic College began to take shape.

At the moment, the campus is spread out in the town of Lander, Wyoming, in the heart of the Rocky Mountains. The college uses space at Holy Rosary Parish, and several other buildings in Lander. The faculty and staff of the college see themselves as putting into action the principles Pope St. John Paul II laid out in his 1990 encyclical on Catholic education, *Ex Corde Ecclesiae*. Wyoming Catholic College seeks "to educate the whole person in mind, spirit, and body through a classical liberal-arts curriculum, aided by a rich Catholic environment and an exciting outdoor leadership program." Part of the college's program to remain authentically Catholic is the administration's refusal to take any federal funds. The college has also founded Saint Michael's Army, with members of the college community as well as their friends and supporters reciting at least once a day the Prayer to St. Michael the Archangel, that by his intercession the college will remain faithful to the Catholic Church and never compromise its independence.

If you are passing through or near Lander, call the college in advance and see if you can schedule a tour and perhaps a conversation with a member of the faculty or student body.

PINE BLUFFS | Our Lady of Peace Shrine
300 Shrine Rd. • Pine Bluffs, WY 82941
307-637-4759 • www.ourladyofpeacewy.com

If you're driving along I-80 in Wyoming, when you reach Pine Bluffs you'll see a giant statue of the Blessed Mother. Standing thirty feet high and weighing 180 tons, this is the tallest sculpture of Our Lady in the United States.

The shrine is the fulfillment of a dream of the Trefen family who, after pilgrimages to many Marian shrines in Europe, were inspired to erect a shrine to Mary that no one driving through the Pine Bluffs area could miss.

Originally, the statue of Mary was the only devotional statue on the grounds. But, since 1998 (when the shrine opened), the donations of pilgrims have enabled the Trefens to add more sacred sculptures to the site.

The shrine, open year-round with free admission, has become the host of an annual pilgrimage, with Mass celebrated outdoors on a stone altar at the base of the statue. Consult the shrine website for the date and time of the next pilgrimage Mass.

ABOUT THE AUTHOR

Thomas J. Craughwell is the author of more than forty books on history, religion, and popular culture, including *Saints Behaving Badly, This Saint Will Save Your Life, St. Peter's Bones,* and *Stealing Lincoln's Body,* which the History Channel produced as a two-hour documentary. He served as the ghostwriter for *Mysteries of the Jesus Prayer,* the companion volume to Norris Chumley's PBS documentary of the same name, and has written articles for the *Wall Street Journal, The American Spectator, U.S. News and World Report, Emmy magazine, Inside the Vatican, National Catholic Register, The Catholic Herald (UK), Reality Magazine (Ireland),* and *Our Sunday Visitor.*